# 15-MINUTE
# CHINESE

## LEARN CHINESE IN JUST 15 MINUTES A DAY

MA CHENG

DORLING KINDERSLEY

London, New York, Munich, Melbourne,
and Delhi

**Senior Editor** Angeles Gavira
**Senior Art Editor** Ina Stradins
**Art Editor** Hugh Schermuly
**Project Editors** Rebecca Warren,
Cathy Meeus, Aakriti Singhal
**Designer** Mitun Banerjee
**DTP Designer** Pushpak Tyagi
**Production Controller** Anna Wilson
**Publishing Manager** Liz Wheeler
**Managing Art Editor** Philip Ormerod
**Managing Editor** Sarah Larter
**Publishing Director** Jonathan Metcalf
**Art Director** Bryn Walls
**Special Photography** Mike Good

Language content for Dorling Kindersley by
g-and-w publishing

First published in Great Britain in 2008 by
Dorling Kindersley Limited
80 Strand, London WC2R 0RL
A Penguin Company
Copyright © 2008 Dorling Kindersley Limited

2 4 6 8 10 9 7 5 3 1

ISBN: 9781405317740

Colour reproduction by Colourscan, Singapore
Printed and bound in China by Leo Paper
Products Limited

See our complete catalogue at
www.dk.com

# Contents

# How to use this book

The main part of the book is devoted to 12 themed chapters, broken down into five 15-minute daily lessons, the last of which is a revision lesson. So, in just 12 weeks you will have completed the course. A concluding reference section contains a menu guide, an English-to-Chinese dictionary, and a guide to Chinese characters.

**Warm up and clock**
Each day starts with a 1-minute warm up that encourages you to recall vocabulary or phrases you have learned previously. A clock to the right of the heading bar indicates the amount of time you are expected to spend on each exercise.

**Useful phrases**
Selected phrases relevant to the topic help you speak and understand.

**Cultural/Conversational tip**
These panels provide additional insights into life in China and language usage.

**Text styles**
Chinese script and pinyin pronunciation (see box opposite) are included, as well as English translation.

**In conversation**
Illustrated dialogues reflecting how vocabulary and phrases are used in everyday situations appear throughout the book.

**How to use the flap**
The book's cover flaps allow you to conceal the Chinese so that you can test whether you have remembered correctly.

**Review and repeat**
A recap of selected elements of previous lessons helps to reinforce your knowledge.

**Instructions**
Each exercise is numbered and introduced by instructions. In some cases, more information is given about the language point being covered.

LEISURE AND SOCIALIZING 123

**Read it**
These panels explain how the Chinese script works, show useful signs, and give tips for deciphering Chinese characters.

**Read it**
Chinese takes basic concepts and combines them to make different meanings, e.g. 飞机 *feiji* "plane" ("flying" 飞 *fei* + "machine" 机 *ji*); 火车 *huoche* "train" ("fire" 火 *huo* + "vehicle" 车 *che*).

**Menu guide**
Identify popular Chinese dishes on the menu with this guide.

## Pinyin pronunciation guide

The Chinese taught in this book is Mandarin Chinese, the main language of the People's Republic of China (PRC). The pronunciation is written in pinyin, the official romanization system used in PRC schools. Most pinyin spellings reflect the nearest equivalent sound in English, but some letters sound different:

a pinyin **x** is pronounced like "sh" as in "ship"
a pinyin **c** is pronounced like "ts" as in "sits"
a pinyin **z** is pronounced like "ds" as in "kids"
a pinyin **q** is pronounced like "ch" as in "chin"
a pinyin **zh** is pronounced like "j" as in "just"
a pinyin **v** is an "u" pronounced with rounded lips, like "few" in English or "über" in German

Mandarin Chinese has four "tones", which affect the way a word is pronounced. Each syllable is pronounced with one of four tones: high, rising, falling–rising, and falling. These tones can be written as accents on the pinyin pronunciation, but you need to listen to and mimic native speakers to master them. Use the *15-Minute Chinese* audio CDs to practise your pronunciation, and the written pinyin as a memory aid.

**Say it**
In these exercises you are asked to apply the vocabulary you have learned in different contexts.

### 5 Say it

Do you have any single rooms?

Two nights.

Is dinner included?

**Dictionary**
A mini-dictionary provides ready reference from English to Chinese for 2,500 words.

138 DICTIONARY

**Dictionary**
*English to Chinese*

This dictionary contains the vocabulary from *15-Minute Chinese*, together with many other high-frequency words. You can also find additional terms for food and drink in the Menu Guide (pp.128–137).

In Chinese, the plural of nouns is normally the same as the singular. Chinese descriptive words, or adjectives, may have different endings depending on how they are used and are also often preceded by *hen* ("very"). Verbs have no tenses and don't generally change according to who or what is the subject, but there are some characters that can be added to indicate a particular time or mood – see p.112.

128 MENU GUIDE

**Menu guide**
This guide lists the most common terms you may encounter on Chinese menus. Dishes are divided into categories and the Chinese script is displayed clearly to help you identify items on a menu.

**1 Warm up**

The Warm up panel appears at the beginning of each topic. Use it to reinforce what you have already learned and to prepare yourself for moving ahead with the new subject.

# Nihao
## *Hello*

Chinese *gongshou* is famous: cupping one hand in the other in front of the chest, which is often accompanied with nodding or a slight bow. Traditionally, there would not be any contact in the form of a handshake or kisses, although this is changing with the increasing Western influence.

**2 Words to remember**

Say these expressions aloud. Hide the text on the left with the cover flap and try to remember the Chinese for each. Check your answers.

| | |
|---|---|
| 早上好。<br>zaoshang hao | *Good morning.* |
| 晚上好。<br>wanshang hao | *Good evening.* |
| 我的名字是…<br>wo-de mingzi shi… | *My name is…* |
| 很高兴认识你。<br>hen gaoxing renshi ni | *Pleased to meet you.* |
| 再见。<br>zaijian | *Goodbye.* |
| 晚安。<br>wan an | *Good night.* |
| 明天见。<br>mingtian jian | *See you tomorrow.* |

你好。
nihao
*Hello!*

**3 In conversation: formal**

你好，我的名字是韩红。
nihao, wo-de mingzi shi
Han Hong

*Hello. My name is Han Hong.*

你好，我的名字是罗伯特·巴克尔。
nihao, wo-de mingzi shi
Luobote Bake'er

*Hello. My name is Robert Barker.*

很高兴认识你。
hen gaoxing renshi ni

*Pleased to meet you.*

## 4 Put into practice

Join in this conversation. Read the Chinese beside the pictures on the left and then follow the instructions to make your reply. Test yourself by concealing the answers with the cover flap.

晚上好。
wanshang hao
*Good evening.*

Say: *Good evening.*

晚上好。
wanshang hao

我的名字是严俊盟。
wo-de mingzi shi Yan Junmeng
*My name is Yan Junmeng.*

Say: *Pleased to meet you.*

很高兴认识你。
hen gaoxing renshi ni

**Conversational tip** The Chinese usually introduce themselves using either just the family name – Han – or the family name followed by the given name – Han Hong. But they are used to hearing Western names the other way: Robert Barker. It's not common to ask someone their name directly, so listen carefully to the introductions. When talking to or about others in an informal situation, "Xiao" or "Lao" is often added in front of their family name depending on whether they are perceived to be younger or older than you. For example, if Han Hong appears younger or more junior, you'd call her/him "Xiao Han"; if older or more senior, "Lao Han" is used to show respect.

## 5 In conversation: informal

明天见。
mingtian jian

*See you tomorrow.*

好，明天见。
hao, mingtian jian

*Yes, see you tomorrow.*

再见。
zaijian

*Goodbye.*

# Wo-de jiating
## *My family*

### 1 Warm up

Say "hello" and "goodbye" in Chinese. (pp.8–9)

Now say "My name is…". (pp.8–9)

Say "Pleased to meet you". (pp.8–9)

Chinese has two sets of vocabulary for many family members, depending on whether you are talking about your own or someone else's. This lesson focusses on speaking about your own family. There's often no need for a separate word meaning *my*: **baba** means *my father*, **gege** *my big brother*, etc.

## 2 Match and repeat

Look at the numbered family members in this scene and match them with the vocabulary list at the side. Read the Chinese words aloud. Now, hide the list with the cover flap and test yourself.

1 奶奶
nainai

2 爷爷
yeye

3 爸爸
baba

4 妈妈
mama

5 儿子
erzi

6 女儿
nv-er

❶ *my grandmother*

❷ *my grandfather*

❸ *my father*

❹ *my mother*

❺ *my son*

❻ *my daughter*

**Conversational tip** Chinese distinguishes between "little" and "big" sister or brother. You will find all the relevant words in section 4. The phrase "xiongdi jiemei" (siblings) is used to refer to your brothers and sisters as a group: "wo you si-ge xiongdi jiemei" (I have four siblings).

### 3  Words to remember: numbers

Memorize these words and then test yourself using the cover flap.

The Chinese use a system of "classifiers" to count specific things. These vary with the nature of what is being counted. The numbers opposite use the near universal classifier 个 **-ge**. You can use this classifier when talking about your family, but it's useful to recognize another classifier 人 **ren** used for people . (Note the alternative character 二 **er** used for the number "two").

| | |
|---|---|
| one | 一个 yi-ge |
| two | 两个 liang-ge |
| three | 三个 san-ge |
| four | 四个 si-ge |
| five | 五个 wu-ge |
| six | 六个 liu-ge |
| seven | 七个 qi-ge |
| eight | 八个 ba-ge |
| nine | 九个 jiu-ge |
| ten | 十个 shi-ge |
| eleven | 十一个 shiyi-ge |
| twelve | 十二个 shi'er-ge |

一人 **yi ren**   1 person
二人 **er ren**   2 people
三人 **san ren**   3 people
四人 **si ren**   4 people
五人 **wu ren**   5 people
六人 **liu ren**   6 people
七人 **qi ren**   7 people
八人 **ba ren**   8 people
九人 **jiu ren**   9 people
十人 **shi ren**   10 people

### 4  Words to remember: relatives

Look at these words and say them aloud. Hide the text on the right with the cover flap and try to remember the Chinese. Check your answers and repeat, if necessary. Then practise the phrases below.

妻
qi
*my wife*

夫
fu
*my husband*

我们是夫妻。
women shi fuqi
*We're married. ("We're husband and wife.")*

| | |
|---|---|
| *my big sister/ my little sister* | 姐姐 / 妹妹 jiejie/meimei |
| *my big brother/ my little brother* | 哥哥 / 弟弟 gege/didi |
| *my siblings* | 兄弟姐妹 xiongdi jiemei |
| *This is my wife.* | 这是我的妻子。 zhe shi wo-de qizi |
| *I have four children.* | 我有四个孩子。 wo you si-ge haizi |
| *We have three daughters.* | 我有三个女儿。 wo you san-ge nv-er |

# Ni-de jiating
## *Your relatives*

### 1 Warm up

Say the Chinese for as many members of (your own) family as you can. (pp.10–11)

Say "I have two sons." (pp.10–11)

Chinese pronouns are straightforward: *I* or *me* is **wo**, *you* is **ni** (or the more formal **nin**), and *he/she* or *him/her* is **ta**. The plural equivalents are made by adding **-men**: *we* **women**, *you* (plural) **nimen**, *they* **tamen**; and the possessives by adding **-de**: *my/mine* **wo-de**, *your/yours* **ni-de**, *their/theirs* **tamen-de**, etc.

## 2 Words to remember

Here are the more respectful terms used to refer to someone else's family, or sometimes to your own in more formal situations.

| | |
|---|---|
| 母亲 muqin | *mother* |
| 父亲 fuqin | *father* |
| 儿子 erzi | *son* |
| 女儿 nv-er | *daughter* |
| 妻子 qizi | *wife* |
| 丈夫 zhangfu | *husband* |
| 孩子 haizi | *children* |
| 兄弟姐妹 xiongdi jiemei | *siblings* |

这是你的母亲吗?
zhe shi ni-de muqin ma
*Is this your mother?*

## 3 In conversation

这是你的丈夫吗?
zhe shi ni-de zhangfu ma

*Is this your husband?*

是的。这是我的父亲。
shi de. zhe shi wo-de fuqin

*That's right. And this is my father.*

你有孩子吗?
ni you haizi ma

*Do you have any children?*

■ **Conversational tip** Forming a question in Chinese is straightforward. Generally, you add the question marker "ma" (吗) to the end of a sentence. "na shi ni-de erzi" (That's your son); "na shi ni-de erzi ma?" (Is that your son?). In very informal spoken Chinese, the question marker is sometimes even dropped "na shi ni-de erzi?"

## 4 Useful phrases

Read these phrases aloud several times and try to memorize them. Conceal the Chinese with the cover flap and test yourself.

| | | |
|---|---|---|
| *Do you have any siblings? (formal)* | 您有兄弟姐妹吗? | nin you xiongdi jiemei ma |
| *Do you have any siblings? (informal)* | 你有兄弟姐妹吗? | ni you xiongdi jiemei ma |

| | | |
|---|---|---|
| *Is this your father?* | 这是你爸爸吗? | zhe shi ni baba ma |
| *Is that your son? (formal)* | 那是您的儿子吗? | na shi nin-de erzi ma |

| | | |
|---|---|---|
| *This is Han Hong's daughter.* | 这是韩红的女儿。 | zhe shi Han Hong de nv-er |
| *Is that your little sister? (informal)* | 那是你妹妹吗? | na shi ni-de meimei ma |

## 5 Say it

Is this your wife?

Is that your little brother?

Do you have a son? (informal)

This is Han Hong's mother.

没有。但我有一个妹妹。
mei you. dan wo you yige meimei

*No, but I have a little sister.*

## 1 Warm up

Say "See you tomorrow." (pp.8–9)

Say "We're married" (pp.10–11) and "Is this your wife?" (pp.12–13)

# Shi/you
## *To be/to have*

The most common verb in Chinese is **shi**, meaning *is, are,* or *am*. The **i** is pronounced only slightly, often making the word sound more like **shuh**. **Shi** does not change with the subject (*I, he, we,* etc.): **wo shi Luobote** (*I'm Robert*), **ta shi yisheng** (*He/she is a doctor*), **women shi zhongguo ren** (*We're Chinese*).

## 2 Useful phrases with shi

Notice that nationalities are expressed by using the name of the country followed by 人 **ren** (*person/people*): **zhongguo ren** *Chinese* (literally *"China land person/people"*), **meiguo ren** *American* (*"America land person/people"*).

| | | |
|---|---|---|
| 我是中国人。<br>wo shi zhongguo ren | *I'm Chinese.* |  |
| 现在是10点钟。<br>xianzai shi shi dianzhong | *It's ten o'clock.* |  |
| 你是医生吗?<br>ni shi yisheng ma | *Are you a doctor?* | |
| 韩红是学生。<br>Han Hong shi xuesheng | *Han Hong is a student.* | |

**Read it** It's not as difficult to begin deciphering the Chinese script as it may appear. *15-Minute Chinese* shows "simplified" characters as used in mainland China. These characters consist of a number of strokes ranging from one to more than twenty (一, 二, 三, 四; one, two, three, four, etc.), similar to how an English word is made up of a number of letters. Some basic concepts are represented by a single character, e.g. 我 **wo** ("I/me"), 人 **ren** ("person"), and these are the common characters you can learn to recognize first. Many other concepts are represented by a combination of characters, e.g. 英国人 **yingguo ren** ("ying-land person", i.e. "English"). You'll find more details on pp.152–9.

我是英国人。
wo shi yingguo ren
*I'm English.*

## 3 Useful phrases: talking about what you have

An informal and straightforward way to talk about possession is to use the expression 有 **you**, meaning *have* or *has*. Learn these phrases and then test yourself by concealing the answers with the cover flap.

| | |
|---|---|
| *I have three children.* | 我有三个孩子。<br>wo you san-ge haizi |
| *My son has a car.* | 我的儿子有车。<br>wo-de erzi you che |
| *I have a little sister.* | 我有一个妹妹。<br>wo you yi-ge meimei |
| *Do you have any children?* | 你有孩子吗?<br>ni you haizi ma |

你有名片吗?
ni you mingpian ma
*Do you have a business card?*

## 4 Negatives

There are two principal ways to make a negative sentence in Chinese: by using the negative markers 不 **bu** or 没 **mei** in front of a verb. **bu** is often used with **shi**, and **mei** with **you**.

| | |
|---|---|
| *We're not American.* | 我们不是美国人。<br>women bu shi meiguo ren |

| | |
|---|---|
| *I don't have a car.* | 我没有车。<br>wo mei you che |

## 5 Put into practice

Join in this conversation. Read the Chinese beside the pictures on the left and then follow the instructions to make your reply. Then test yourself by concealing the answers with the cover flap.

晚上好。
wanshang hao
*Good evening.*

*Say: Good evening. I'm Robert.*

晚上好, 我是罗伯特。
wanshang hao, wo shi Luobote

很高兴认识你。
hen gaoxing renshi ni
*Pleased to meet you.*

*Ask: Do you have a business card?*

你有名片吗?
ni you mingpian ma

# Fuxi yu lianxi
## *Review and repeat*

**Da an**
*Answers*
Cover with flap

### 1 How many?

### 1 How many?

Hide the answers with the cover flap. Then say these Chinese numbers aloud. Check that you have remembered the Chinese correctly.

1 三
  san

2 九
  jiu

3 四
  si

4 二
  er

5 八
  ba

6 十
  shi

7 五
  wu

8 七
  qi

9 六
  liu

### 2 Hello

### 2 Hello

You meet someone in a formal situation. Join in the conversation, replying in Chinese following the English prompts.

1 你好，我的名字
  是 …
  nihao, wo-de
  mingzi shi …

nihao, wo-de mingzi shi Yan Junmeng
1 *Answer the greeting and give your name.*

2 很高兴认识你。
  hen gaoxing
  renshi ni

zhe shi wo-de qizi
2 *Say "Pleased to meet you."*

3 我有三个儿子。
  你有孩子吗?
  wo you san-ge
  erzi. ni you haizi
  ma

ni you haizi ma
3 *Say "I have three sons.
  Do you have any children?"*

4 再见。
  zaijian

mei you. dan wo you yi-ge didi
4 *Say "Goodbye."*

## 3 Be or have

Fill in the blanks with **shi** (*to be*) or **you** (*to have*). Then check your answers carefully.

1 wo _____ zhongguo ren

2 wo _____ san-ge erzi

3 women _____ yingguo ren

4 Sarah _____ yisheng

5 ni _____ haizi ma

6 ta bu _____ xuesheng

7 wo-de mingzi
   _____ Han Hong

8 women mei _____
   che

### 3 Be or have

1 是
  shi

2 有
  you

3 是
  shi

4 是
  shi

5 有
  you

6 是
  shi

7 是
  shi

8 有
  you

## 4 Family

Say the Chinese for each of the numbered family members. Check your answers carefully.

❶ *my grandmother*

❷ *my grandfather*

*my father* ❸

❹ *my daughter*   ❻ *my mother*

❺ *my son*

### 4 Family

1 奶奶
  nainai

2 爷爷
  yeye

3 爸爸
  baba

4 女儿
  nv-er

5 儿子
  erzi

6 妈妈
  mama

**1 Warm up**

Count up to ten.
(pp.10–11)

Remind yourself how
to say "hello" and
"goodbye." (pp.8–9)

Ask "Do you have
any children?"
(pp.14–15)

# Zai kafei ting
*In the café*

You will find different types of cafés
in China: there are traditional types,
which are called **chaguan**; and
Western-style coffee houses, simply
called **kafei ting**. These modern cafés
are very popular, particularly amongst
young Chinese.

**Cultural tip** The generic word for tea is
"cha". Three popular types are "lvcha" (green tea –
popular in eastern China), "hongcha" (red tea – southern
China), and "huacha" (jasmine tea – northern China).

## 2 Words to remember

Look at the words below and say them out
loud a few times. Conceal the Chinese with
the cover flap and try to remember each one
in turn. Also practise the words on the right.

奶茶
naicha
*tea with milk*

| 绿茶<br>lvcha | *green tea* |
|---|---|
| 红茶<br>hongcha | *red tea* |
| 花茶<br>huacha | *jasmine tea* |
| 三明治<br>sanmingzhi | *sandwich* |

## 3 In conversation

请给我一杯咖啡。
qing geiwo yibei kafei

*I'd like a coffee.*

还要其它食品吗？
haiyao qita shipin ma

*Anything else?*

有蛋糕吗？
you dangao ma

*Do you have any
cakes?*

## 4 Useful phrases

Learn these phrases. Read the English under the pictures and say the phrase in Chinese as shown on the right. Then cover up the answers on the right and test yourself.

蛋糕
dangao
*cake*

请给我一杯咖啡。
qing geiwo yibei kafei

*I'd like a coffee.*

还要其它食品吗?
haiyao qita shipin ma

*Anything else?*

糖
tang
*sugar*

还要一块蛋糕。
haiyao yi kuai dangao

*A cake, too, please.*

多少钱?
duo shao qian

*How much is that?*

咖啡
kafei
*coffee*

有,当然有。
you, dangran you

*Yes, certainly.*

还要一块蛋糕。
多少钱?
haiyao yi kuai dangao.
duo shao qian

*A cake, too, please.*
*How much is that?*

50元… 谢谢你。
wushi yuan... xiexie ni

*That's 50 yuan...*
*thank you.*

## 1 Warm up

Say "A coffee, please."
(pp.18–19)

Say "I don't have a
car." (pp.14–15)

Ask "Do you have any
cakes?" (pp.18–19)

# Zai canguan
## *In the restaurant*

There are different types of eating
places in China. You can find snacks or
a light meal at street stalls. A **fanguan**
serves traditional Chinese food.
Department stores often house relaxed
**canting** *(canteens)* on the upper floors,
open until about 10pm and serving
both international and Chinese dishes.

## 2 Words to remember

Familiarize yourself with these words and
test yourself using the flap.

| | |
|---|---|
| 菜单<br>caidan | *menu* |
| 酒水单<br>jiushui dan | *wine list* |
| 头盘<br>toupan | *starters* |
| 主食<br>zhushi | *main courses* |
| 甜点<br>tiandian | *desserts* |
| 早餐<br>zaocan | *breakfast* |
| 午餐<br>wucan | *lunch* |
| 晚餐<br>wancan | *dinner* |

hand towel **7**

chopsticks **6**

**4** fork

**5** spoon

## 3 In conversation

请给我们安排一张四
人餐桌。
qing geiwomen anpai yi
zhang si ren canzhuo

*We'd like a table
for four.*

你们有预订吗?
nimen you yuding ma

*Do you have a
reservation?*

有。是巴克尔预订的。
you. shi Bake'er yuding
de

*Yes, I do. In the name
of Barker.*

## 4 Match and repeat

Look at the numbered items in this table setting and match them with the Chinese words on the right. Read the Chinese words aloud. Now, conceal the Chinese with the cover flap and test yourself.

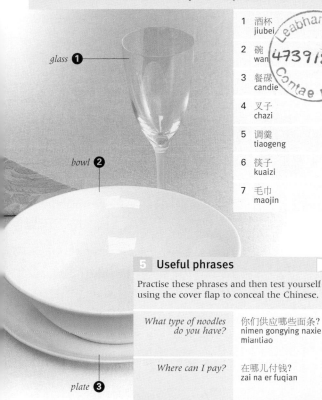

*glass* **1**

*bowl* **2**

*plate* **3**

1 酒杯
   jiubei

2 碗
   wan

3 餐碟
   candie

4 叉子
   chazi

5 调羹
   tiaogeng

6 筷子
   kuaizi

7 毛巾
   maojin

## 5 Useful phrases

Practise these phrases and then test yourself using the cover flap to conceal the Chinese.

| | |
|---|---|
| *What type of noodles do you have?* | 你们供应哪些面条?<br>nimen gongying naxie mianliao |
| *Where can I pay?* | 在哪儿付钱?<br>zai na er fuqian |

你们想要抽烟区还是
非抽烟区?
nimen xiang yao chouyan
qu haishi fei chouyan qu

*Would you like smoking
or non-smoking?*

我们想要非抽烟区。
women xiang yao fei
chouyan qu

*We'd like non-
smoking.*

好吧，这边请。
haoba, zhebian qing

*Very well. Here you are.*

### 1 Warm up

Say "We're married"
(pp.10–11) and "I'm
English." (pp.14–15)

Ask "Do you have any
siblings?" (pp.12–13)

Say "A sandwich,
please." (pp.18–19)

# Caiyao
## *Dishes*

A typical meal in China consists of rice
and a soup, together with a variety of
fish, meat, and vegetable dishes. The
meal is served with pickles and other
condiments such as raw spring onions
and chilli sauce depending on the
region. Alcohol is consumed before
the rice or noodles are served.

**Cultural tip** "Taocan" (set menus) are popular,
particularly at lunchtime. These consist of a soup, rice,
pickles, and other dishes – all presented on a tray.
"Gaijiaofan" (rice with toppings) are a simpler alternative.

### 2 Match and repeat

Look at the numbered items and match them to the Chinese words
in the panel on the left.

1 水果
  shuiguo

2 蔬菜
  shucai

3 面条
  miantiao

4 海鲜
  haixian

5 汤
  tang

6 肉
  rou

7 鱼
  yu

8 蘑菇
  mogu

9 米饭
  mifan

❶ fruit

❽ mushrooms

❾ rice

❺ soup

❼ fish

❻ meat

### 3 Words to remember: cooking methods

Familiarize yourself with these words.

你们供应哪些肉?
nimen gongying naxie rou
*What type of meat
do you have?*

| | | |
|---|---|---|
| *fried* | 炒 | chao |
| *grilled* | 烧 | shao |
| *roasted* | 烤 | kao |
| *boiled* | 煮 | zhu |
| *steamed* | 蒸 | zheng |
| *raw* | 生吃 | shengchi |

### 6 Say it

What's "Nuomi"?

I'd like a baijiu.

What type of fish do you have?

### 4 Words to remember: drinks

Familiarize yourself with these words.

| | | |
|---|---|---|
| *water* | 水 | shui |
| *mineral water* | 矿泉水 | kuangquanshui |
| *"baijiu" (Chinese liquor/spirit)* | 白酒 | baijiu |
| *wine* | 葡萄酒 | putaojiu |
| *beer* | 啤酒 | pijiu |
| *fruit juice* | 果汁 | guozhi |

❷ *vegetables*

*noodles* ❸

❹ *seafood*

### 5 Useful phrases

Practise these phrases and then test yourself.

| | |
|---|---|
| *I'd like a beer.* | 请给我一杯啤酒。 qing geiwo yibei pijiu |
| *I'm vegetarian.* | 我是素食者。 wo shi sushizhe |
| *I'm allergic to nuts.* | 我对坚果过敏 wo dui jianguo guomin |
| *What's "Qianzhang"?* | 什么是千张? shenme shi qianzhang |

## 1 Warm up

What are "breakfast", "lunch", and "dinner" in Chinese? (pp.20–1)

Say "I'm vegetarian" and "I'd like a fruit juice" in Chinese. (pp.22–3)

# Qingqiu
## *Requests*

You've learned two common phrases that are used for asking for something: **qing geiwo...** *(I'd like...)* and **qing geiwomen...** *(We'd like...).* Alternatively, you can say what you want followed by **hao ma** *(please)*: **wo yao... hao ma** *(I want..., please).* You can use this phrase in almost any situation.

## 2 Basic requests

Here are some phrases for making basic requests in Chinese using **qing geiwo/geiwomen...** and **wo yao... hao ma.** Learn these phrases and then test yourself by using the cover flap.

| | |
|---|---|
| 我要一个蛋糕，好吗?<br>wo yao yige dangao,<br>hao ma | *I want a cake, please.* |
| 我要一个叉子，好吗?<br>wo yao yige chazi,<br>hao ma | *I want a fork, please.* |
| 请给我一杯茶<br>qing geiwo yibei cha | *I'd like a tea.* |
| 请给我们安排一张<br>三人餐桌。<br>qing geiwomen anpai yi<br>zhang san ren canzhuo | *We'd like a table for<br>for three.* |
| 请给我菜单。<br>qing geiwo caidan | *I'd like the menu.* |
| 我要一点糖果，好吗?<br>wo yao yidian tangguo,<br>hao ma | *I want some sweets,<br>please.* |
| 给我加满，好吗?<br>geiwo jia man, hao ma | *Fill it up, please.*<br>("A full tank,<br>please.") |

请给我接王先生的
电话。
qing geiwo jie Wang
xiansheng de dianhua
*I'd like to speak to
Mr Wang.*

**■ Read it** Some Chinese characters are simple and resemble the item they describe, such as the character for "people": 人 (ren). The PRC simplified the characters, although traditional versions are still used in some of the Chinese-speaking areas. The sign on the left is simplified characters, which say **tingzhi yingye** meaning "business stopped", or "closed".

## 3 Polite requests

In a business situation, you may want to appear ultra-polite by using
the polite version of "you" – **nin** instead of **ni** – especially if talking to
someone senior. Learn these phrases and then test yourself.

*Would you please
help me?*

请您帮帮我，好吗?
qing nin bangbang wo,
hao ma

*Could I have your
signature here,
please?*

请您在这里签名，
好吗?
qing nin zai zheli
qianming, hao ma

*Could I have your
phone number,
please?*

请把您的电话号码给
我，好吗?
qing ba nin-de dianhua
haoma geiwo, hao ma

## 4 Put into practice

Join in this conversation. Read the Chinese beside the pictures
on the left and then follow the instructions to make your reply
in Chinese. Test yourself by hiding the answers with the cover flap.

晚上好。你们有预订
吗?
wanshang hao. nimen
you yuding ma
*Good evening. Do you
have a reservation?*

没有。请给我们安排
一张三人餐桌。
mei you. qing
geiwomen anpai yi
zhang san ren canzhuo

*Say: No. We'd like a
table for three.*

您想喝什么饮料?
nin xiang he shenme
yinliao
*What would you
like to drink?*

请给我一杯啤酒。
qing geiwo yibei pijiu

*Say: I'd like a beer.*

# Fuxi yu lianxi
*Review and repeat*

**Da an**
*Answers*
Cover with flap

### 1 What food?

1 汤
tang

2 蔬菜
shucai

3 鱼
yu

4 肉
rou

5 酒杯
jiubei

6 米饭
mifan

### 1 What food?

Name the numbered items.

**1** soup
**2** vegetables
**3** fish
**4** meat
glass **5**

### 2 This is my...

1 这是我的丈夫。
zhe shi wo-de zhangfu

2 这是我的女儿。
zhe shi wo-de nv-er

3 他们是我的兄弟姐妹。
tamen shi wo-de xiongdi jiemei

### 2 This is my...

Say these phrases in Chinese.

1 *This is my husband.*

2 *This is my daughter.*

3 *These are my siblings.*

### 3 I'd like...

1 请给我一个蛋糕
qing geiwo yige dangao

2 请给我一点糖
qing geiwo yidian tang

3 请给我一杯咖啡
qing geiwo yibei kafei

4 请给我一杯茶
qing geiwo yibei cha

### 3 I'd like...

Say "I'd like" the following:

cake **1**
**4** tea
sugar **2**
coffee **3**

**6** rice

chopsticks **7**

**8** noodles

beer **10**

**9** hand towel

## 1 What food?

7 筷子
kuaizi

8 面条
miantiao

9 毛巾
maojin

10 啤酒
pijiu

## 4 Restaurant

You arrive at a restaurant. Join in the conversation, replying in Chinese wherever you see the English prompts.

wanshang hao
1 *Ask "Do you have a table for three?"*

nimen you yuding ma
2 *Say "Yes, we do. In the name of Barker."*

nimen xiang yao chouyan qu haishi fei chouyan qu
3 *Say "We'd like non-smoking."*

haoba. zhebian qing
4 *Say "We'd like the menu, please."*

haiyao qita shipin ma
5 *Ask "Do you have a wine list?"*

## 4 Restaurant

1 有三个人的桌子吗?
you san-ge ren de zhuozi ma

2 有。是巴克尔预定的。
you. shi Bake'er yuding de

3 我们想要非抽烟区。
women xiang yao fei chouyan qu

4 请给我们菜单,好吗?
qing geiwomen caidan, hao ma

5 有酒水单吗?
you jiushui dan ma

## 1 Warm up

How do you say "I have four children"? (pp.10–11)

Now say "We're not English" and "I don't have a car." (pp.14–15)

What is Chinese for "my mother"? (pp.10–11)

# Riqi he yuefen
## *Days and months*

The most important holiday of the year is the one-week Chinese New Year, which usually happens in early February. Two other long holidays are May 1st (International Labour Day) and October 1st (Chinese National Day), which also last for five days. Christmas isn't generally celebrated.

## 2 Words to remember: days of the week

Familiarize yourself with these words and test yourself using the flap.

| | | |
|---|---|---|
| 星期一 xingqiyi | *Monday* | |
| 星期二 xingqier | *Tuesday* | |
| 星期三 xingqisan | *Wednesday* | |
| 星期四 xingqisi | *Thursday* |  明天见。 mingtian jian *We meet tomorrow.* |
| 星期五 xingqiwu | *Friday* | |
| 星期六 xingqiliu | *Saturday* | |
| 星期日 xingqiri | *Sunday* | |
| 今天 jintian | *today* | |
| 明天 mingtian | *tomorrow* |  我今天有预订。 wo jintian you yuding *I have a reservation for today.* |
| 昨天 zuotian | *yesterday* | |

## 3 Useful phrases: days

There is no Chinese equivalent of *on* or *in*, as in *on Tuesday, in February*.

| | | |
|---|---|---|
| 会议不是星期二。 huiyi bu shi xingqier | *The meeting isn't on Tuesday.* |  |
| 我星期日工作。 wo xingqiri gongzuo | *I work on Sundays.* | |

## 4 Words to remember: months of the year

Chinese months are named simply "1 month", "2 month", etc.

| | | |
|---|---|---|
| | *January* | 一月<br>yiyue |
| | *February* | 二月<br>eryue |
| | *March* | 三月<br>sanyue |
| | *April* | 四月<br>siyue |
| | *May* | 五月<br>wuyue |
| | *June* | 六月<br>liuyue |
| | *July* | 七月<br>qiyue |
| | *August* | 八月<br>bayue |
| | *September* | 九月<br>jiuyue |
| | *October* | 十月<br>shiyue |
| | *November* | 十一月<br>shiyiyue |
| | *December* | 十二月<br>shieryue |
| | *next month* | 下个月<br>xiageyue |
| | *last month* | 上个月<br>shanggeyue |

我们的结婚周年是
七月。
women-de jiehun
zhounian shi qiyue
*Our anniversary is
in July.*

中国春节是二月。
zhongguo chuanjie shi
eryue
*Chinese New Year is
in February.*

## 5 Useful phrases: months

Learn these phrases and then test yourself using the cover flap.

| | | |
|---|---|---|
| | *My children are on holiday in August.* | 我的孩子八月放假。<br>wo-de haizi bayue fangjia |
| | *My birthday is in June.* | 我的生日是六月。<br>wo-de shengri shi liuyue |

## 1 Warm up

Count in Chinese from one to twelve.
(pp.10–11)

Say "Do you have a reservation?"
(pp.20–1)

Say "The meeting isn't on Wednesday."
(pp.28–9)

# Shijian he shuzi
## *Time and numbers*

When telling the time in Chinese, the hour comes first, for example, **yidian** (*one o'clock*), **jiudian** (*nine o'clock*), etc., followed by the minutes: **wufen** (*five minutes*), **shifen** (*ten minutes*). Ban is "a half" (*30 minutes*), **yike** "a quarter" (*15 minutes*), and **sanke** "three-quarters"(*45 minutes*).

## 2 Words to remember: time

Memorize how to tell the time in Chinese.

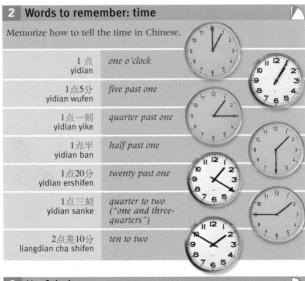

| | |
|---|---|
| 1 点<br>yidian | one o'clock |
| 1点5分<br>yidian wufen | five past one |
| 1点一刻<br>yidian yike | quarter past one |
| 1点半<br>yidian ban | half past one |
| 1点20分<br>yidian ershifen | twenty past one |
| 1点三刻<br>yidian sanke | quarter to two ("one and three-quarters") |
| 2点差10分<br>liangdian cha shifen | ten to two |

## 3 Useful phrases

Learn these phrases and then test yourself using the cover flap.

| | |
|---|---|
| 现在几点了?<br>xianzai ji dian le | What time is it? |
| 你几点想吃早餐?<br>ni ji dian xiang chi zaocan | At what time do you want breakfast? |
| 我有一个12点的预订。<br>wo you yige shier dian de yuding | I have a reservation for twelve o'clock. |

## 4 Words to remember: higher numbers

Chinese numbers are very logical. To count above ten, the individual numbers are simply added together. So 11 is **shiyi** *("ten-one")*, 15 is **shiwu** *("ten-five")*, etc. Be careful, though, to put the numbers the right way around: **wushi** is 50 *("five-ten")*, **qishi** is 70 *("seven-ten")*. Units are added directly after the tens: 68 is **liushi ba**; 25 is **ershi wu**, and so on.

Pay special attention to the number 10,000, which is **wan** or **yiwan**. A million is **yibaiwan** *("one hundred-ten thousands")*.

这是五百元。
zhe shi wubai yuan
*That's 500 yuan.*

## 5 Say it

twenty-five

ninety-two

seven hundred

twenty thousand

five to ten

half past eleven

That's 75 yuan.

| | | |
|---|---|---|
| *eleven* | 十一 | shiyi |
| *twelve* | 十二 | shier |
| *thirteen* | 十三 | shisan |
| *fourteen* | 十四 | shisi |
| *fifteen* | 十五 | shiwu |
| *sixteen* | 十六 | shiliu |
| *seventeen* | 十七 | shiqi |
| *eighteen* | 十八 | shiba |
| *nineteen* | 十九 | shijiu |
| *twenty* | 二十 | ershi |
| *thirty* | 三十 | sanshi |
| *forty* | 四十 | sishi |
| *fifty* | 五十 | wushi |
| *sixty* | 六十 | liushi |
| *seventy* | 七十 | qishi |
| *eighty* | 八十 | bashi |
| *ninety* | 九十 | jiushi |
| *one hundred* | 一百 | yibai |
| *three hundred* | 三百 | sanbai |
| *one thousand* | 一千 | yiqian |
| *ten thousand* | 一万 | yiwan |
| *two hundred thousand* | 二十万 | ershiwan |
| *one million* | 一百万 | yibaiwan |

## 1 Warm up

Say the days of the week. (pp.28–9)

Say "three o'clock." (pp.30–1)

What is "today", "tomorrow", and "yesterday" in Chinese? (pp.28–9)

# Yuyue
## *Appointments*

There's no fundamental difference when it comes to making an appointment and meeting someone for the first time. If it's a business meeting, people do exchange business cards first. When you do so, remember to hand over your business card with both hands.

## 2 Useful phrases

Learn these phrases and then test yourself.

| | |
|---|---|
| 我们明天见，好吗?<br>women mingtian jian, hao ma | *Shall we meet tomorrow?* |
| 和谁?<br>he shei | *With whom?* |
| 您什么时候有空?<br>nin shenme shihou you kong | *When are you free?* |
| 对不起，那天我很忙。<br>duibuqi, na tian wo hen mang | *Sorry, I'm busy that day.* |
| 星期四怎么样?<br>xingqisi zenmeyang | *How about Thursday?* |
| 对我正合适。<br>dui wo zheng heshi | *That's good for me.* |

欢迎。
huanying
*Welcome.*

## 3 In conversation

你好，我有预约。
nihao, wo you yuyue

*Hello. I have an appointment.*

和谁?
he shei

*With whom?*

与王先生。
yu Wang xiansheng

*With Mr Wang.*

## 4 Put into practice

Practise these phrases. Then cover up the text on the right and say the answering part of the dialogue in Chinese. Check your answers and repeat if necessary.

我们星期四见面，好吗?
women xingqisi jianmian, hao ma
*Shall we meet on Thursday?*

Say: Sorry, I'm busy that day.

对不起，那天我很忙。
duibuqi, na tian wo hen mang

您什么时候有空?
nin shenme shihou you kong
*When are you free?*

Say: On Tuesday in the afternoon.

星期二下午我有空。
xingqier xiawu wo you kong

对我正合适。
dui wo zheng heshi
*That's good for me.*

Ask: At what time?

什么时间呢?
shenme shijian ne

**Read it** It's useful to recognize some common Chinese signs you might see around a building. The signs below are a combination of characters. The final character in each (处 *chu*) means "place" or "location".

接待处 jie dai chu (reception)　　问讯处 wen xun chu (information desk)

很好。约的是什么时间?
henhao. yue de shi shenme shijian

*Very good. What time is the appointment?*

十点钟。
shidian zhong

*At ten o'clock.*

请坐吧。
qing zuo bai

*Take a seat, please.*

## 1  Warm up

How do you say
"sorry"? (pp.32–3)

Ask "Shall we meet
tomorrow?" (pp.32–3)

Say "I'd like a cake,
please." (pp.24–5)

# Da dianhua
## *On the telephone*

The Chinese usually answer the
telephone with **wei** (*hello*), although
sometimes **nihao** can also be used. You
should not use **wei** for face-to-face
greetings. Almost all public telephones
have English instructions and work
with phonecards (**dianhua ka** or **IP ka**)
available at most stores.

## 2  Match and repeat

Match the numbered items to the Chinese
in the panel on the left and test yourself.

1  充电器
   chongdianqi

2  留言机
   liuyanji

3  电话机
   dianhuaji

4  电话卡
   dianhua ka

5  手机
   shouji

6  耳机
   erji

*charger* **1**

**3** *telephone*

*earphones* **6**

**5** *mobile*

## 3  In conversation

喂，我是总机。
wei, wo shi zongji

*Hello, operator
speaking. ("I am
the operator.").*

喂, 请给我接王先生的
电话。
wei, qing geiwo jie Wang
xiansheng de dianhua

*Hello, I'd like to speak
to Mr Wang.*

您是谁呀?
nin shi shei ya

*Who's calling?*

## 4 Useful phrases

Practise these phrases. Then test yourself using the cover flap.

请给我接外线。
qing geiwo jie waixian

*I'd like an outside line.*

我要买电话卡，好吗？
wo yao mai dianhua ka, hao ma
*I want to buy a phonecard, please.*

请给我接王先生的电话。
qing geiwo jie Wang xiansheng de dianhua

*I'd like to speak to Mr Wang, please.*

**2** answering machine

我可以给他留言吗？
wo keyi gei ta liuyan ma

*Can I leave a message?*

**4** phonecard

对不起，我打错电话了。
duibuqi, wo da cuo dianhua le

*Sorry, I have the wrong number.*

我是大通印刷厂的张兴良。
wo shi datong yinshua chang de Zhang Xingliang

*I'm Zhang Xingliang from Tatong Printing.*

对不起，电话占线。
duibuqi, dianhua zhanxian

*I'm sorry, the line is busy.*

可不可以让王先生给我回电话？
ke bu keyi rang Wang xiansheng geiwo hui dianhua

*Can you ask Mr Wang to call me back?*

# Fuxi yu lianxi
*Review and repeat*

## 1 Sums

1 十六
shiliu

2 三十九
sanshijiu

3 五十三
wushisan

4 七十八
qishiba

5 九十九
jiushijiu

6 十七
shiqi

## 1 Sums

Speak out loud the answers to these sums in Chinese. Then check your answers.

1 $10 + 6 = ?$

2 $14 + 25 = ?$

3 $66 - 13 = ?$

4 $40 + 38 = ?$

5 $90 + 9 = ?$

6 $20 - 3 = ?$

## 3 Telephones

What are the numbered items in Chinese?

*mobile* ❶

*phonecard* ❸

## 2 To want

1 请
qing

2 好
hao

3 茶
cha

4 给我
geiwo

5 我
wo

6 电话
dianhua

## 2 To want

Fill the gaps in these requests with the correct word.

1 _____ geiwo yibei pijiu

2 wo yao yige dangao, _____ ma

3 qing geiwo yibei nai_____

4 qing _____ jie waixian

5 _____ yao mai dianhua ka, hao ma

6 qing geiwo jie Wang xiansheng de _____

**Da an**
*Answers*
Cover with flap

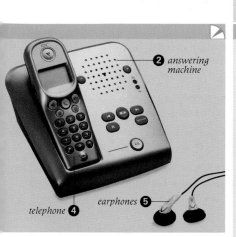

② *answering machine*

*telephone* ④   *earphones* ⑤

## 3 Telephones

1 手机
shouji

2 留言机
liuyanji

3 电话卡
dianhua ka

4 电话机
dianhuaji

5 耳机
erji

## 4 When?

What do these sentences mean?

1 mingtian jian

2 wo xingqiliu gongzuo

3 wo de shengri shi wuyue

4 wo jintian you dingtai

## 4 When?

1 *We meet/see you tomorrow.*

2 *I work on Saturday.*

3 *My birthday is in May.*

4 *I have a reservation for today.*

## 5 Time

Say these times in Chinese.

## 5 Time

1 1点
yidian

2 1点5分
yidian wufen

3 1点20分
yidian ershifen

4 1点半
yidian ban

5 1点一刻
yidian yike

6 2点差10分
liangdian cha shifen

## 1 Warm up

Count to 100 in tens.
(pp.10–11 and
pp.30–1)

Ask "What time is it?"
(pp.30–1)

Say "half past one".
(pp.30–1)

# Zai huoche zhan
## *At the train station*

Each type of train service in China has a unique reference. This consists of an English letter followed by a number, which indicates the route and class. Generally, services beginning with Z are the fastest, non-stop trains, while K or T indicates express long-distance trains, stopping only at major stations.

## 2 Words to remember

Learn these words and then test yourself.

乘客
chengke
*passenger*

出入口
churukou
*entry/exit*

| | |
|---|---|
| 车站<br>chezhan | *station* |
| 火车<br>huoche | *train* |
| 站台<br>zhantai | *platform* |
| 车票<br>chepiao | *ticket* |
| 单程票<br>danchengpiao | *single* |
| 往返票<br>wangfanpiao | *return* |
| 硬卧车厢<br>yingwo chexiang | *sleeper coach* |
| 普通车厢<br>putong chexiang | *ordinary coach* |

车站很拥挤。
chezhan hen yongji
*The station is crowded.*

## 3 In conversation

我想买两张去北京的
车票。
wo xiang mai liangzhang
qu Beijing de chepiao

*Can I buy two tickets to Beijing, please?*

往返票吗?
wangfanpiao ma

*Is that return?*

是的。我需要确定座
位吗?
shi de. wo xuyao
queding zuowei ma

*Yes. Do I need to make seat reservations?*

## 4 Useful phrases

Learn these phrases and then test yourself using the cover flap.

| | |
|---|---|
| *How much is a ticket to Shanghai?* | 去上海的车票多少钱？<br>qu shanghai de chepiao duo shao qian |
| *Can I use a credit card?* | 可以用信用卡吗？<br>keyi yong xinyongka ma |
| *Do I have to change?* | 需要换车吗？<br>xuyao huanche ma |
| *Which platform does the train leave from?* | 从第几站台上车？<br>cong di ji zhantai shangche |
| *What time does the train leave?* | 火车几点发车？<br>huoche ji dian fa che |

去上海的火车晚点了。
qu shanghai de huoche wandian le
*The train for Shanghai is late.*

### 5 Say it

The train is crowded.

How much is a ticket to Beijing?

**Cultural tip** You can normally buy your rail tickets in advance from your hotel by paying a small handling fee. If this service is not available at your hotel, you can visit a travel agency or the station to buy tickets. You will need to pay in cash at the station. There are a few places where you can buy tickets from a machine.

不需要。总共100元。
bu xuyao. zonggong yibai yuan

*No. That's 100 yuan.*

可以用信用卡吗？
keyi yong xinyongka ma

*Can I use a credit card?*

我们只收现金。请从第一站台上车。
women zhi shou xianjin. qing cong di yi zhantai shangche

*We only take cash. The train leaves from platform one.*

## 1 Warm up

How do you say "train"? (pp.38–9)

What are "tomorrow" and "yesterday" in Chinese? (pp.28–9)

Count from 10 to 20. (pp.30–1)

# Qu/cheng
## *To go/to take*

Qu (*to go*) and **cheng** (*to take*) are essential verbs you will need as you find your way around. Chinese verbs do not change according to the subject or tense as they do in English (*I go, you went*, etc.). A verb generally appears immediately after the subject, or "doer", of the action.

## 2 Qu/cheng: to go/to take

Read these phrases aloud several times and try to memorize them. Conceal the Chinese with the cover flap and test yourself.

| | |
|---|---|
| 你去哪儿?<br>ni qu na'er | *Where are you going?<br>(informal)* |
| 您要去哪儿?<br>nin yao qu na'er | *Where are you going?<br>(formal)* |
| 我去火车站。<br>wo qu huoche zhan | *I'm going to the station.* |
| 我乘地铁上班。<br>wo cheng ditie shangban | *I take the under-ground to work.* |
| 我乘出租车上班。<br>wo cheng chuzuche shangban | *I take a taxi to work.* |
| 我要乘公共汽车去。<br>wo yao cheng gonggong qiche qu | *I want to go by bus.* |

今天我去长城。
jintian wo qu changcheng
*Today I'm going to the Great Wall.*

**Cultural tip** Taxis in China have signs clearly marked in both Chinese characters and English. Most of the major cities have ample taxis cruising the main streets and they are usually easy to hail. Otherwise, the hotel can order one. Fares are very reasonable by Western standards. Tipping is not customary, as it isn't in most service situations in China.

## 3 Past and future

The character 了 **le** or 过 **guo** immediately after a verb shows it is in the past: **qu le** or **qu guo** *(went/have been to)*. There is no special form for the future; the verb is used with a time indicator, e.g. **mingtian** *(tomorrow)*.

| | *I took a taxi.* | 我乘了出租车。<br>wo cheng le chuzuche |

| | *I went to the Great Wall.* | 我去了长城。<br>wo qu le changcheng |

| | *Tomorrow, I'll take the underground to work.* | 明天我乘地铁上班。<br>mingtian wo cheng ditie shangban |

| | *Tomorrow, I'll take the bus to work.* | 明天我乘公共汽车上班。<br>mingtian wo cheng gonggong qiche shangban |

## 4 Put into practice

Cover the text on the right and complete the dialogue in Chinese.

| | 你去哪儿？<br>ni qu na'er<br>*Where are you going?* | 我去火车站。<br>wo qu huoche zhan |
| | *Say: I'm going to the train station.* | |

| | 你要乘地铁吗？<br>ni yao cheng ditie ma<br>*Do you want to take the underground?* | 不，我要乘公共汽车。<br>bu, wo yao cheng gonggong qiche |
| | *Say: No, I want to take the bus.* | |

| | 你需要乘120路公共汽车。<br>ni xuyao cheng yibai ershi lu gonggong qiche<br>*That'll be bus number 120.* | 谢谢你。<br>xiexie ni |
| | *Say: Thank you.* | |

Say "I want to go by bus." (pp.40–1)

Ask "Where are you going?" (pp.40–1)

What's 88 in Chinese? (pp.30–1)

# Gonggong qiche, chuzuche, ditie
*Bus, taxi, and underground*

On buses, you can generally buy your ticket from a machine as you get on board. In smaller cities, you can buy your tickets from a bus conductor.

## 2 Words to remember

Familiarize yourself with these words.

| 公共汽车<br>gonggong qiche | *bus* |
| 出租车<br>chuzuche | *taxi* |
| 地铁<br>ditie | *underground* |
| 公共汽车站<br>gonggong qiche zhan | *bus station* |
| 出租车站<br>chuzuche zhan | *taxi rank* |
| 地铁站<br>ditie zhan | *underground station* |
| 车票<br>chepiao | *ticket* |
| 路<br>lu | *line/route* |

518路车在这儿停吗?
wubaiyishiba lu che zai zhe er ting ma
*Does the number 518 stop here?*

## 3 In conversation: taxi

请带我去故宫, 好吗?
qing daiwo qu gugong, hao ma

*I'd like to go to the Forbidden City, please.*

上车吧。
shangche ba

*Do get in.*

我就在这儿下车, 可以吗?
wo jiu zai zhe er xiache, keyi ma

*Can you drop me here, please?*

## 4 Useful phrases

Learn these phrases and then test yourself using the cover flap.

*I'd like a taxi to Dongdan, please.*

请给我叫出租车去东单，好吗？
qing geiwo jiao chuzuche qu dongdan, hao ma

*What time is the next bus to the airport?*

下一趟去机场的公共汽车几点发车？
xiayitang qu jichang de gonggong qiche ji dian fa che

*How do you get to the Summer Palace?*

去颐和园怎么走？
qu yiheyuan zenme zou

*Please wait for me.*

请等等我。
qing dengdeng wo

---

### Cultural tip

Beijing and Shanghai have extensive metro systems. Station names can be recognized by a sign (as shown here), in both pinyin and Chinese. Fares are very reasonable.

### 6 Say it

I'd like to go to the Summer Palace, please.

I'd like a taxi to the Forbidden City.

How do you get to Dongdan?

---

## 5 In conversation: bus

这趟车去故宫博物院吗？
zhe tang che qu gugong bowuyuan ma

*Is this bus going to the Palace Museum?*

是的。不很远。
shide. bu hen yuan

*Yes. It's not very far.*

到了那里，您能告诉我吗？
dao le nall, nln neng gaosu wo ma

*Can you tell me when to get off?*

## 1 Warm up

How do you say "I'd like a coffee, please"? (pp.14–15)

Say "my father", "my sister", and "my parents". (pp.12–13)

Say "I'm going to the Great Wall." (pp.40–1)

# Jia che
## *On the road*

There's a growing number of cars in Chinese cities and on the expressways. The road systems are expanding fast. Renting a car is not as unusual or difficult as it once was, although issues with licences and the crowded and unfamiliar roads make it preferable to also hire a driver.

## 2 Match and repeat

Match the numbered items to the list on the left, then test yourself.

1 挡风玻璃
  dangfengboli

2 发动机盖
  fadongjigai

3 保险杠
  baoxiangang

4 车胎
  chetai

5 前灯
  qiandeng

6 车门
  chemen

7 车轮
  chelun

8 后舱
  houcang

9 后视镜
  houshijing

**Cultural tip** Traffic in China moves on the right. The growing network of expressways is fast and efficient, but outside Beijing tolls are generally payable.

1 *windscreen*
2 *bonnet*
3 *bumper*
4 *tyre*
5 *headlights*

## 3 Road signs

单向行车道
danxiang xingche dao

*One way traffic*

出口
chukou

*Exit*

最大时速
xuida shisu

*Maximum speed*

## 4 Useful phrases

Learn these phrases and then test yourself using the cover flap.

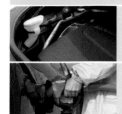

| | | |
|---|---|---|
| | *The engine won't start.* | 发动机无法启动。<br>fadongji wufa qidong |
| | *Fill it up, please.* | 请加满油箱。<br>qing jiaman you xiang |

## 5 Words to remember

Familiarize yourself with these words then test yourself using the flap.

### 6 Say it

Oil, please.

The car won't start.

**9** wing mirror

**8** boot

**6** door

**7** wheel

| | | |
|---|---|---|
| *car* | 汽车 | qiche |
| *driving licence* | 驾照 | jiazhao |
| *petrol* | 汽油 | qiyou |
| *oil* | 柴油 | chaiyou |
| *engine* | 发动机 | fadongji |
| *flat tyre* | 车胎没气了 | chetai meiqi le |

**Read it** Road signs are often written in Chinese characters only. If you're driving, familiarize yourself with the Chinese script for your destination, as well as the more common signs, such as 停 **ting** ("stop").

停
ting

*Stop*

禁止进入
jinzhi jinru

*No entry*

禁止停车
jinzhi tingche

*No parking*

# Fuxi yu lianxi
## *Review and repeat*

### 1 Transport

1 出租车
chuzuche

2 自行车
zixingche

3 汽车
qiche

4 地铁
ditie

5 公共汽车
gonggong qiche

### 1 Transport

Name these forms of transport
in Chinese.

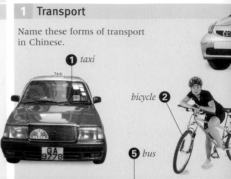

**1** *taxi*

*bicycle* **2**

**5** *bus*

### 2 Go and take

1 去
qu

2 哪儿
na'er

3 站
zhan

4 上班
shangban

5 了/过
le/guo

6 乘
cheng

### 2 Go and take

Use the correct Chinese word to fill the gaps.

1 jintian wo _____ changcheng

2 nin yao qu _____

3 wo qu huoche _____

4 wo cheng ditie qu _____

5 (zuotian) wo cheng _____ chuzuche

6 wo yao _____ gonggong qiche qu

**3** car

underground **4**

### 3 Questions

How do you ask these questions in Chinese?

1 *"Do you have any cakes?"*

2 *"Do you have any children?"*

3 *"What time is it?"*

4 *"What time does the train leave?"*

5 *"Where are you going?"* *(informal).*

6 *"Can I use a credit card?"*

### 3 Questions

1 有蛋糕吗?
you dangao ma

2 你有孩子吗?
ni you haizi ma

3 现在几点了?
xianzai ji dian le

4 火车几点发车?
huoche ji dian fa che

5 你去哪儿?
ni qu na'er

6 可以用信用卡吗?
keyi yong xinyongka ma

### 4 Tickets

You're buying tickets at a train station. Join in the conversation, replying in Chinese following the numbered English prompts.

zaoshang hao
1 *Can I buy two tickets to Shanghai, please?*

wangfanpiao ma
2 *No. I want singles.*

zonggong yibai yuan
3 *What time does the train leave?*

ni ji jippun mae desu
4 *Which platform does the train leave from?*

qing cong di yi zhantai shangche
5 *Thank you.*

### 4 Tickets

1 我想买两张去上海的车票。
wo xiang mai liangzhang qu shanghai de chepiao

2 不, 我要单程票。
bu, wo yao danchengpiao

3 火车几点发车?
houche ji dian fa che

4 从第几站台上车?
cong di ji zhantai shangche

5 谢谢你。
xiexie ni

## 1 Warm up

Ask "Do you go to the museum?" (pp.42–3)

What are "station" and "ticket" in Chinese? (pp.38–9)

# Zai chengshi nei
## *About town*

To talk about features or facilities, you can use the word **you**. Earlier, we learned that **you** means *have/has*, but it can also mean *there is/are*. The opposite is **mei you**. Notice the word order in Chinese: **daqiao fujin you youyongchi** = *bridge/near to/there is/swimming pool* (*There's a swimming pool near the bridge*).

## 2 Match and repeat

Match the numbered locations to the words in the panel.

1 斑马线
  banmaxian

2 停车场
  tingchechang

3 喷泉
  penquan

4 百货大楼
  baihuodalou

5 广场
  guangchang

6 博物馆
  bowuguan

7 电影院
  dianyingyuan

8 大桥
  daqiao

**①** *crossing*

**②** *car park*

**③** *fountain*

**⑧** *bridge*

## 3 Words to remember

Familiarize yourself with these words and test yourself using the cover flap.

| | |
|---|---|
| 加油站 **jiayouzhan** | *petrol station* |
| 旅游服务中心 **lvyou fuwu zhongxin** | *tourist information centre* |
| 游泳池 **youyongchi** | *swimming pool* |
| 网吧 **wangba** | *internet café* |

**⑦** *cinema*

## 4 Useful phrases

Learn these phrases and then test yourself using the cover flap.

| | | |
|---|---|---|
| | *Is there a museum nearby?* | 附近有博物馆吗？<br>fujin you bowuguan ma |
| | *Is it far from here?* | 离这里远吗？<br>li zheli yuan ma |
| | *There's a swimming pool near the bridge.* | 大桥附近有游泳池。<br>daqiao fujin you youyongchi |
| | *There isn't a tourist information centre.* | 没有旅游服务中心。<br>mei you lvyou fuwu zhongxin |

宝塔在市中心。
baota zai shi zhongxin
*The pagoda is in the centre of town.*

④ *department store*

⑤ *square*

## 5 Put into practice

Join in this conversation. Read the Chinese on the left and follow the instructions to make your reply. Then test yourself by concealing the answers with the cover flap.

没有问题吧？
mei you wenti ba
*Is everything OK?*

*Ask: Is there an internet café nearby?*

附近有网吧吗？
fujin you wangba ma

没有，但是有一个旅游服务中心。
mei you, danshi you yi-ge lvyou fuwu zhongxin
*No there isn't, but there's a tourist information centre.*

*Ask: Is it far from here?*

离这里远吗？
li zheli yuan ma

靠近火车站。
kaojin huoche zhan
*It's near the train station.*

*Say: Thank you.*

谢谢你。
xiexie ni

⑥ *museum*

## 1  Warm up

How do you say "bridge" and "fountain"? (pp.48–9)

Ask "Is it far from here?" (pp.48–9)

Ask "Is there a museum in town?" (pp.48–9)

# Wen lu
## *Asking directions*

Finding your way around a town in China can be confusing, so it is a good idea to learn how to ask for and understand directions. Chinese street names are written in characters along with pinyin transcription, so it's useful to familiarize yourself with both for your convenience.

## 2  Useful phrases

Practise these phrases and then test yourself.

| | |
|---|---|
| 左 / 右转。<br>zuo/you zhuan | *Turn left/right.* |
| 在左边。<br>zai zuobian | *On the left.* |
| 在右边。<br>zai youbian | *On the right.* |
| 照直走。<br>zhaozhi zou | *Go straight on.* |
| 请问, 去宝塔怎么走?<br>qingwen, qu baota zenme zou | *Excuse me, how do I get to the pagoda?* |
| 第一个街口, 在左边。<br>diyi ge jiekou, zai zuobian | *First street on the left.* |
| 第二个街口, 在右边。<br>dier ge jiekou, zai youbian | *Second street on the right.* |

公园
gongyuan
*park*

办公楼
bangonglou
*office block*

走到街角, 左转。
zou dao jiejiao, zuo zhuan
*At the corner, turn left.*

## 3  In conversation

请问, 城里有餐馆吗?
qingwen, chengli you canguan ma

*Excuse me, is there a restaurant in town?*

有, 靠近火车站。
you, kaojin huoche zhan

*Yes there is, near the train station.*

去火车站怎么走?
qu huoche zhan zenme zou

*How do I get to the train station?*

## 4 Words to remember

Familiarize yourself with these words and test yourself using the flap.

我迷路了。
wo milu le
*I'm lost.*

| | | |
|---|---|---|
| *traffic lights* | 红绿灯 | hong lv deng |
| *street corner* | 街角 | jiejiao |
| *street* | 街 | jie |
| *road* | 路 | lu |
| *map* | 地图 | ditu |
| *flyover* | 立交桥 | lijiaoqiao |
| *opposite* | 对面 | duimian |
| *at the end of the street* | 这条街走到底 | zhe tiao jie zoudaodi |

我们在哪里?
women zai nali
*Where are we?*

## 5 Say it

At the traffic lights, turn right.

At the station, turn left.

It's about ten minutes.

到了交通灯，左转
daole hong lv deng, zuo zhuan

*At the traffic lights, turn left.*

远吗?
yuan ma

*Is it far?*

不远。大概五分钟
buyuan. dagai wufen zhong

*No, it's about five minutes.*

Say the days of the week in Chinese. (pp.28–9)

How do you say "six o'clock"? (pp.30–1)

Ask "What time is it?" (pp.30–1)

# Guanguang
## *Sightseeing*

Chinese shops are open late every day, closing around 10 or 11pm and they operate seven days a week. Tourist sights such as museums are usually open all day from about 8am, but may be closed during the lunch hour and for one day a week, although this is not always the case.

## 2 Words to remember

Familiarize yourself with these words and test yourself using the flap.

| | |
|---|---|
| 导游册<br>daoyou ce | *guidebook* |
| 免费(入场)<br>mianfei (ruchang) | *free (entrance)* |
| 门票<br>menpiao | *admission ticket* |
| 禁止拍照<br>jinzhi paizhao | *cameras not allowed* |
| 休息<br>xiuxi | *closed* |

团体参观
tuanti canguan
*guided tour*

---

**Cultural tip** China is a vast country, with its major cities growing so fast that sightseeing often requires a lot of advance planning. Internal flights can be arranged to take you between the different regions, but you will need permits to visit some areas and it is best to check this out locally before you set off.

---

## 3 In conversation

你们今天下午开门吗?
nimen jintian xiawu
kaimen ma

*Do you open this
afternoon?*

是的, 但我们六点钟关
门。
shide, dan women
liudian zhong guanmen

*Yes, but we close at
six o'clock.*

轮椅可以方便进出
吗?
lunyi keyi fangbian
jinchu ma

*Is wheelchair access
possible?*

## 4  Useful phrases

Learn these phrases and then test yourself using the cover flap.

| | What time do you open? | 你们什么时间开门?<br>nimen shenme shijian kaimen |
| | What time do you close? | 你们什么时间关门?<br>nimen shenme shijian guanmen |
| | Is wheelchair access possible? | 轮椅可以方便进出吗?<br>lunyi keyi fangbian jinchu ma |

## 5  Put into practice

Cover the text on the right and complete the dialogue in Chinese.

对不起, 博物馆关门了。
duibuqi, bowuguan guanmen le
*Sorry, the museum is closed.*

*Ask: Do you open on Sundays?*

你们星期天开门吗?
nimen xingqitian kaimen ma

是的, 但是关门时间比较早。
shide, danshi guanmen shijian bijiaozao
*Yes, but we close early.*

*Ask: What time do you close?*

你们什么时间关门?
nimen shime shijian guanmen

可以, 那边有电梯。
keyi, na bian you dianti

*Yes, there's a lift over there.*

谢谢, 我要买四张门票。
xiexie, wo yao mai si zhang menpiao

*Thank you. I'd like to buy four tickets.*

这是您的门票, 导游册免费。
zhe shi nin-de menpiao, daoyou ce mianfei

*Here are your tickets. The guidebook is free.*

# Zai jichang
## *At the airport*

International flights arrive at most major cities, and there is an extensive network of internal flights operating from every provincial capital. Although the airport environment is largely universal, it is sometimes useful to be able to understand key words and phrases in Chinese.

## 2 Words to remember

Familiarize yourself with these words and test yourself using the flap.

| | |
|---|---|
| 办理登 手续<br>banli dengji shouxu | *check-in* |
| 出发<br>chufa | *departures* |
| 到达<br>daoda | *arrivals* |
| 海关<br>haiguan | *customs* |
| 边防检查<br>bianfang jiancha | *passport control* |
| 候机楼<br>houjilou | *terminal* |
| 登机口<br>dengjikou | *gate* |
| 航班<br>hangban | *flight* |
| 飞机<br>feiji | *plane* |

哪个登机口去香港?
na ge dengjikou qu xianggang
*Which gate is it for Hong Kong?*

## 3 Useful phrases

Learn these phrases and then test yourself using the cover flap.

| | |
|---|---|
| 去伦敦的飞机准点吗?<br>qu lundun de feiji zhundian ma | *Is the plane to London on time?* |
| 我找不到我的行李。<br>wo zhao bu dao wo-de xingli | *I can't find my baggage.* |
| 去上海的飞机晚点了。<br>qu shanghai de feiji wandian le | *The plane to Shanghai is delayed.* |

## 4 Put into practice

Join in this conversation. Read the Chinese on the left and follow
the instructions to make your reply. Then test yourself by concealing
the answers with the cover flap.

下一位。
xiayiwei
*Next, please.*

*Ask: Is the plane to
Shanghai on time?*

去上海的飞机准点
吗?
qu shanghai de feiji
zhundian ma

Airlines check-in area

是的, 准点。
shide, zhundian
*Yes, it's on time.*

*Ask: Which gate is it?*

哪个登机口?
na ge dengjikou

## 5 Match and repeat

Match the numbered items to the Chinese words in the panel.

boarding **1**
pass

ticket **2**

passport **3**

**4** suitcase

**5** trolley

1 登机牌
dengjipai

2 机票
jipiao

3 护照
huzhao

4 箱子
xiangzi

5 手推车
shoutuiche

### Read it

Chinese takes basic
concepts and
combines them
to make different
meanings, e.g.
飞机 *feiji* "plane"
("flying" 飞 *fei* +
"machine" 机 *ji*);
火车 *huoche* "train"
("fire" 火 *huo* +
"vehicle" 车 *che*).

**Da an**
*Answers*
Cover with flap

# Fuxi yu lianxi
*Review and repeat*

## 1 Places

1 博物馆
bowuguan

2 斑马线
banmaxian

3 大桥
daqiao

4 宝塔
baota

5 停车场
tingchechang

6 电影院
dianyingyuan

7 广场
guangchang

## 1 Places

Name the numbered places in Chinese.

❶ *museum*  ❷ *crossing*  ❸ *bridge*

❹ *pagoda*  ❺ *car park*

❻ *cinema*

❼ *square*

## 2 Car parts

1 挡风玻璃
dangfengboli

2 前灯
qiandeng

3 保险杠
baoxiangang

4 车门
chemen

5 车胎
chetai

## 2 Car parts

Name these car parts in Chinese.

*windscreen* ❶

❺ *tyre*  *door* ❹

## 3 Translation

What do these Chinese phrases mean?

1 zhuan zuo

2 cheng li you bowuguan ma

3 mei you wangba

4 women zai nali

5 daqiao fujin you youyongchi

6 nimen shenme shijian kaimen

7 wo yao mai si zhang menpiao

### 3 Translation

1 *Turn left.*

2 *Is there a museum in town?*

3 *There isn't an internet café.*

4 *Where are we?*

5 *There's a swimming pool near the bridge.*

6 *What time do you open?*

7 *I'd like four tickets.*

## 4 Directions

Ask how to get to these places:

1 *pagoda*

2 *train station*

3 *internet café*

4 *cinema*

❷ *headlight*

❸ *bumper*

### 4 Directions

1 去宝塔怎么走?
qu baota zenme zou

2 去火车站怎么走?
qu huoche zhan zenme zou

3 去网吧怎么走?
qu wangba zenme zou

4 去电影院怎么走?
qu dianyingyuan zenme zou

## 1 Warm up

Ask "How much is that?" (pp.18–19)

What are "breakfast", "lunch", and "dinner"? (pp.20–1)

What are "three", "four", "five", and "six"? (pp.10–11)

# Ding fangjian
## *Booking a room*

Large and medium-sized cities have a considerable number of international hotels as well as traditional Chinese spas. Most hotels are star-rated, and Western tourists will generally find that hotels with a minimum of a three-star rating will meet their expected standards.

## 2 Useful phrases

Practise these phrases and then test yourself by concealing the Chinese on the left with the cover flap.

| | | |
|---|---|---|
| 房价包含早餐吗?<br>fangjian baohan<br>zaocan ma | *Is breakfast included?*<br>*(Does the room*<br>*include breakfast?)* |  |
| 房间里能上网吗?<br>fangjian li neng<br>shangwang ma | *Does the room have*<br>*internet access?* |  |
| 有送餐服务吗?<br>you songcan fuwu ma | *Is there room service?* |  |
| 最迟几点钟退房?<br>zuichi jidianzhong tuifa | *What time is*<br>*check out?* |  |

## 3 In conversation

有空房间吗?
you kong fangjian ma

*Do you have*
*any rooms?*

有。我们有一间双人房。
you. women you yijian
shuangren fang

*Yes, we have a*
*double room.*

有送餐服务吗?
you songcan fuwu ma

*Is there room service?*

## 4 Words to remember

Familiarize yourself with these words and test yourself by concealing the Chinese on the right with the cover flap.

房间里能看到海景吗?
fangjian li neng kandao
haijing ma
*Does the room have
a sea view?*

| | | |
|---|---|---|
| *room* | 房间 | fangjian |
| *single room* | 单人房 | danren fang |
| *double room* | 双人房 | shuangren fang |
| *lift* | 电梯 | dianti |
| *bathroom* | 卫生间 | weishengjian |
| *shower* | 淋浴 | linyu |
| *breakfast* | 早餐 | zaocan |
| *key* | 钥匙 | yaoshi |
| *balcony* | 阳台 | yangtai |
| *two nights* | 两天 | liangtian |
| *three nights* | 三天 | santian |

## 5 Say it

Do you have any
single rooms?

Two nights.

Is dinner included?

**Cultural tip** Chinese hotel rooms tend to include a pair of house slippers as a matter of course. You are assumed to want to remove your shoes in the room as you would at home. Tooth-brushes and toothpaste are also provided.

有。您要住几天?
you. nin yao zhu jitian

*Yes, there is. How
many nights?*

三天。
santian

*Three nights.*

好了。这是您的钥匙。
haole. zhe shi nin-de
yaoshi

*Very good. Here's
your key.*

# Zai jiudian
*In the hotel*

## 1 Warm up

How do you say "Is/Are there...?", "There is/are...", and "There isn't/aren't...?" (pp.48–9)

What's the Chinese for "room"? (pp.58–9)

Most of the new hotels designed for foreign tourists and business people are modelled on standard international hotel chains. Those rated three-star or above usually provide a broadband internet connection in the room, free of charge.

## 2 Match and repeat

Match the numbered items in this hotel bedroom with the Chinese text in the panel and test yourself using the cover flap.

1 床头柜
 chuangtougui

2 电灯
 diandeng

3 窗帘
 chuanglian

4 沙发
 shafa

5 枕头
 zhentou

6 床
 chuang

7 床单
 chuangdan

8 毛毯
 maotan

**①** *bedside table*    **③** *curtains*

**②** *lamp*

*sofa* **④**

**⑤** *pillow*

**⑥** *bed*

**⑦** *bedspread*

*blanket* **⑧**

**Cultural tip** It's common to find a flask of hot water in your room to make tea or simply drink by itself. Room service should be able to refill the flask if it runs out. Bottled water is also sometimes provided free of charge. In common with most international hotels, hotels in China add a surcharge for using the telephone.

## 3 Useful phrases

Learn these phrases and then test yourself using the cover flap.

The room is too hot.

房间里太热。
fangjian li tai re

The room is too cold.

房间里太冷。
fangjian li tai leng

There aren't any towels.

没有毛巾了。
mei you maojin le

I'd like some soap.

我要一块肥皂。
wo yao yikuai feizao

The shower is broken.

淋浴坏了。
linyu huai le

## 4 Put into practice

Cover the text on the right and then complete the dialogue in Chinese.

你好，我是前台。
nihao, wo shi qiantai
Hello, this is the front desk.

没有枕头了。
mei you zhentou le

Say: There aren't any pillows.

工作人员很快就会给您送去。
gongzuo renyuan hen kuai jiu hui gei nin songqu
The staff will bring you some.

还有，房间里太热。
haiyou, fangjian li tai re

Say: And also, the room is too hot.

# Wenquan dujia
*Hot spas*

## 1 Warm up

What is Chinese for "shower" (pp.60–1), and "swimming pool"? (pp.48–9)

Say "I'd like some towels." (pp.60–1)

Many tourist spots in China feature **wenquan dujia** (*hot spas*), combined with accommodation at times. You can experience traditional Chinese beauty and healing treatments, which emphasize the balance between **yin** and **yang** and advocate natural ways to boost **qi** (vitality inside the body).

## 2 Match and repeat

Learn these words and then test yourself by concealing the Chinese with the cover flap.

1 阳伞
yangsan

2 晨衣
chenyi

3 蜡烛
lazhu

4 床旗
chuangqi

5 拖鞋
tuoxie

6 足疗
zuliao

❷ *dressing gown*

*parasol* ❶

❻ *foot treatment*   ❺ *slippers*

## 3 In conversation

有哪些疗法呢?
you na xie liaofa ne

*What kind of treatments are there?*

可以做按摩，也可以洗温泉浴。
keyi zuo anmo, ye keyi xi wenquan yu

*You can have a massage or a hot spa bath.*

一次需要多长时间?
yici xuyao duochang shijian

*How long will the treatment take?*

## 4 Useful phrases

Learn these phrases. Read the English under the pictures and say the phrase in Chinese as shown on the right. Then cover up the answers on the right and test yourself.

一次需要多长时间？
yici xuyao duochang shijian

*How long will the treatment take?*

可以针灸吗？
keyi zhenjiu ma

*Can I have acupuncture?*

可以药物洗脚吗？
keyi yaowu xijiao ma

*Can I have a herbal foot massage?*

这草药味道很香。
zhe caoyao weidao henxiang

*These herbs are fragrant.*

## 5 Say it

Can I have a hot spa bath?

What kind of massages are there?

I'd like a foot massage.

**3** *candle*

*bed runner* **4**

有一小时的，也有两小时的。
you yi xiaoshi de, ye you liang xiaoshi de

*There are one-hour or two-hour (sessions).*

很贵吗？
hen gui ma

*Is it very expensive?*

不贵，一小时350元。
bu gui, yixiao shi sanbai wushi yuan

*It's not expensive, 350 yuan per hour.*

# Xingrongci
## *Adjectives*

Basic adjectives (descriptive words) are quite straightforward in Chinese: *car(s)* is **qiche**; *small car(s)* is **xiao qiche**. A simple way to describe things is to use the word **hen,** which carries the meaning of *very*: **zhe qiche hen xiao** *"This car is (very) small",* **shan hen gao** *"The mountains are (very) high".*

## 2 Words to remember

There are no plurals in Chinese. So "the mountain is (very) high" and "the mountains are (very) high" would both be **shan hen gao.**

| | |
|---|---|
| 大<br>da | *big, large* |
| 小<br>xiao | *small* |
| 高<br>gao | *high, tall* |
| 低<br>di | *low* |
| 热<br>re | *hot* |
| 冷<br>leng | *cold* |
| 安静<br>anjing | *quiet* |
| 吵闹<br>chaonao | *noisy* |
| 硬<br>ying | *hard* |
| 软<br>ruan | *soft* |
| 美<br>mei | *beautiful* |

宝塔很古老。
baota hen gulao
*The pagoda is (very) old.*

树很美。
shu hen mei
*The trees are (very) beautiful.*

## ■ Read it

The first two adjectives above – 大 da, "big", and 小 xiao, "small" – are amongst the easiest Chinese characters to recognize. They originate from representations of a person holding arms out wide ("big") and pointing down by the side ("small"). These characters combine with others, for example 小鼠 xiao-shu means "mouse" ("small rat"); 大衣 da-yee means "coat" ("big jacket").

## 3 Useful phrases

Learn these useful descriptive phrases and then test yourself using the cover flap.

*The coffee is cold.*

咖啡冷了。
kafei leng le

*My room is very noisy.*

我的房间很吵闹。
wo-de fangjian hen chaonao

*This car is very small.*

这汽车很小。
zhe qiche hen xiao

*This bed is very hard.*

这床很硬。
zhe chuang hen ying

## 4 Put into practice

Join in this conversation. Cover up the text on the right and complete the dialogue in Chinese. Check and repeat if necessary.

房间在这里。
fangjian zai zheli
*Here's the room.*

Say: *The view is very beautiful.*

景色很美。
jingse hen mei

卫生间在那里。
weishengjian zai nali
*The bathroom is over there.*

Say: *The room is very small.*

房间很小。
fangjian hen xiao

可惜，没有其他房间了。
kexi, mei you qita fangjian le
*Unfortunately, there aren't any other rooms.*

Say: *We'll take it.*

我们就要它。
women jiu yao ta

**Da an**
*Answers*
Cover with flap

# Fuxi yu lianxi
*Review and repeat*

### 1 Adjectives

1 大
  da

2 软
  ruan

3 古老
  gulao

4 安静
  anjing

5 冷
  leng

## 1 Adjectives

Put the word in brackets into Chinese.

1 zhe qiche hen _____ **(big)**

2 zhe chuang hen ying _____ **(soft)**

3 baota hen _____ **(old)** ma

4 wo-de fangjian hen _____ **(quiet)**

5 cha _____ **(cold)** le

### 2 Spas

1 足疗
  zuliao

2 拖鞋
  tuoxie

3 阳伞
  yangsan

4 晨衣
  chenyi

5 蜡烛
  lazhu

6 床旗
  chuangqi

## 2 Spas

Name these items you might find in a traditional Chinese spa.

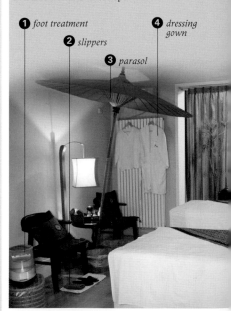

❶ *foot treatment*

❷ *slippers*

❸ *parasol*

❹ *dressing gown*

## 3 At the hotel

You are booking a room in a hotel. Follow the conversation, replying in Chinese using the English prompts.

nihao
1 *Do you have any rooms?*

nin yao zhu jitian
2 *Five nights.*

haole
3 *Is breakfast included?*

fangjian baohan zaocan
4 *We'll take it.*

## 3 At the hotel

1 有空房间吗?
you kong fangjian ma

2 五天。
wutian

3 房价包含早餐吗?
fangjian baohan zaocan ma

4 我们就要它。
women jiu yao ta

**5** *candle*

*bed runner* **6**

## 4 Negatives

Make these sentences negative using **bu** or **mei**.

1 wo shi zhongguo ren

2 wo you san-ge haizi

3 fujin you wangba

4 Han Hong shi xuesheng

5 women you kafei

## 4 Negatives

1 我不是中国人。
wo bu shi zhongguo ren

2 我没有三个孩子。
wo mei you san-ge haizi

3 附近没有网吧吗?
fujin mei you wangba ma

4 韩红不是学生。
Han Hong bu shi xuesheng

5 我们没有咖啡。
women mei you kafei

## 1 Warm up

Ask "Can I use a credit card?" (p.39)

Say "At the traffic lights, turn left ", and "The station is near the café." (pp.50–1)

# Baihuo shangdian
## *Department store*

Department stores are sometimes referred to as **baihuodalou** (*"big building department stores"*) since they tend to be landmark buildings in city centres, selling everything from clothes to musical instruments. The concept is changing as shopping malls have mushroomed in many Chinese cities.

## 2 Match and repeat

Notice the Chinese word 类 lei, meaning *category*: **juilei**, *spirit category (off-licence)*; **yulei**, *fish category (fishmonger)*, etc. Match the shops below to the Chinese words in the panel on the left.

1 面包类
mianbaolei

2 糕点类
gaodianlei

3 酒类
jiulei

4 类
shushilei

5 蔬菜类
shucailei

6 图书类
tushulei

7 鱼类
yulei

8 肉类
roulei

9 豆制品类
douzhipinlei

❶ baker

❷ cake shop

❹ delicatessen

❺ greengrocer

❼ fishmonger

❽ butcher

**Cultural tip** Department stores are a good place to look for gifts to take home and often have a folk art section ("gongyipinlei"). Here you can buy traditional souvenirs, from sandalwood fans to embroideries and vases. Most of the large stores will also be able to accept credit cards — something you can't rely on in smaller shops.

## 3 Words to remember

Familiarize yourself with these words and then test yourself.

|  |  |
|---|---|
| *dairy* | 乳制品<br>ruzhipin |
| *antique shop* | 古董店<br>gudongdian |
| *hairdresser* | 美发店<br>meifadian |
| *barber* | 理发店<br>lifadian |
| *jeweller* | 珠宝店<br>zhubaodian |
| *post office* | 邮局<br>youju |
| *florist* | 花卉店<br>huahuidian |
| *shoe shop* | 鞋店<br>xiedian |
| *travel agent* | 旅行社<br>lvxingshe |

哪里有花卉店?
nali you huahuidian
*Can you tell me where the florist is?*

**3** off-licence

**6** bookshop

**9** tofu shop

## 4 Useful phrases

Familiarize yourself with these phrases.

| | |
|---|---|
| *Can you tell me where the hairdresser is?* | 哪里有美发店?<br>nali you meifadian |
| *Where can I pay?* | 在哪里付钱?<br>zai nali fuqian |
| *I'm just looking, thanks.* | 我只想看看，谢谢。<br>wo zhixiang kankan,<br>xiexie |
| *Where can I buy phonecards?* | 哪里可以买到电话<br>卡?<br>nali keyi maidao<br>dianhua ka |
| *Can I exchange this?* | 我可以更换它吗?<br>wo keyi genghuan ta ma |
| *I'd like a receipt, please?* | 请给我一张发票，<br>好吗?<br>qing gei wo yizhang<br>fapiao, hao ma |
| *I'd like to place an order for...* | 我想订购一个...<br>wo xiang dinggou<br>yige... |

## 5 Say it

Can you tell me where the baker is?

Where can I buy fish?

I'd like to place an order for curtains.

What are "forty", "seventy", "a hundred", "a thousand", and "ten thousand" in Chinese? (pp.30–1)

Say "big" and "small" in Chinese. (pp.64–5)

# Dianqi shangdian
## *Electronics store*

The Chinese are catching up with the West, in terms of electrical and electronic consumer goods. In every mall and large department store, there's bound to be a store or department selling computers, mobile phones, digital cameras, etc. Power rates in China are 220V/50Hz.

## 2  Match and repeat

Match the numbered items to the Chinese words in the panel on the left and test yourself using the cover flap.

1 鼠标
shubiao

2 适配器
shipeiqi

3 变压器
bianyaqi

4 笔记本电脑
bijiben diannao

5 屏幕
pingmu

6 保修证
baoxiuzheng

7 内存
neicun

8 电池
dianchi

> **Read It** When you see price labels, you will usually see the symbol for "yuan" ¥ followed by the price in Western figures or sometimes the price followed by the Chinese character 元.
>
> ¥5800          50 元

**1** *mouse*   *transformer* **3**

*adapter* **2**

*memory* **7**

**8** *battery*   *guarantee* **6**

## 3  In conversation

这台笔记本电脑多少钱?
zhe tai bijiben diannao duo shao qian

*How much is that laptop computer?*

5800元。
wuqian babai yuan

*It's 5,800 yuan.*

硬盘空间有多大?
yingpan kongjian youduoda

*How big is the hard drive?*

🇨🇳 **Cultural tip** The Chinese currency is called "Renminbi" (literally "people's money") and the unit is the yuan. The highest denomination banknote is 100 yuan. Although this may not seem like a large amount when you exchange currency, 100 yuan can still go a long way in China.

**④** laptop
**⑤** screen

### 4 Useful phrases

Learn these phrases. Then conceal the answers on the right using the cover flap. Read the English under the pictures and say the phrase in Chinese as shown on the right.

这架相机太贵。
zhe jia xiangji tai gui

*That camera is too expensive.*

这款多少钱?
zhe kuan duo shao qian

*How much is that one?*

这架相机太贵。

在英国能用吗?
zai yingguo neng yong ma

*Will it work in England?*

40吉兆, 1吉兆的内存。
sishi jizhao, yi jizhao de neicun

*40 gigabytes, and one gigabyte of memory.*

在英国能用吗?
zai yingguo neng yong ma

*Will it work in England?*

能用。但是需要一个变压器。
neng yong. sanshi xuyao yige bianyaqi

*Yes it will, but you need a transformer.*

## 1 Warm up

What are these items which you could buy in a supermarket? (pp.22–3)

shuiguo
mifan
shucai
miantiao
yu
rou

# Chaoji shichang
## *At the supermarket*

In recent years, many multinational supermarket operators have entered the Chinese market. Familiar names can be found in every large and medium-sized city in China.
The layout is similar to Western supermarkets but with a blend of Chinese and imported goods available.

## 2 Match and repeat

Look at the numbered items and match them to the Chinese words in the panel on the left.

1 饮料
yinliao

2 化妆品
huazhuangpin

3 小吃
xiaochi

4 冷冻食品
lengdongshipin

5 蔬菜
shucai

6 即食食品
jishishipin

7 家庭用品
jiatingyongpin

8 水果
shuiguo

*drinks* ❶

*fruit* ❽

*household products* ❼

*ready meals* ❻

*vegetables* ❺

❹ *frozen foods*

**■ Cultural tip** Supermarkets usually pre-package fresh produce such as meat, fish, fruit, vegetables, and soybean products. You just pick up the pre-priced packet you want and take it to the checkout counter.

## 3 Useful phrases

Learn these phrases and then test yourself using the cover flap.

| | |
|---|---|
| *I'd like a bag, please.* | 请给我一个塑料袋, 好吗? <br> qing geiwo yige suliaodai, hao ma |
| *Where is the drinks section?* | 饮料在什么地方? <br> yinliao zai shenme defang |
| *Where's the checkout counter?* | 在哪儿付款? <br> zai na'er fukuan |
| *Where are the shopping trolleys?* | 哪儿有手推车? <br> na'er you shoutuiche |

## 4 Words to remember

Learn these words and then test yourself using the cover flap.

❷ beauty products

❸ snacks

| | | |
|---|---|---|
| *bread* | 面包 | mianbao |
| *milk* | 牛奶 | niunai |
| *butter* | 黄油 | huangyou |
| *dairy products* | 乳制品 | ruzhipin |
| *ham* | 火腿 | huotui |
| *salt* | 盐 | yan |
| *pepper* | 胡椒 | hujiao |
| *toilet paper* | 卫生纸 | weishengzhi |
| *nappies* | 尿片 | nlaoplan |
| *washing-up liquid* | 洗洁精 | xijiejing |

## 5 Say it

Where is the snacks section?

I'd like some butter, please?

Is there any ham?

## 1 Warm up

Say "I'd like a...,
please." (pp.24–5)

Ask "Is there a...?"
(pp.48–9)

Say "thirteen",
"twenty-four", and
"thirty." (pp.30–1)

Say "big" and
"small." (pp.64–5)

# Yifu he xiezi
## *Clothes and shoes*

A vast variety of clothing to suit all
styles and budgets is now available in
China, both in the clothing sections
of shopping centres and department
stores and in local markets. Except in
some of the more rural areas, the
traditional dress is now mainly seen
only in films and at the Chinese opera.

## 2 Match and repeat

Match the numbered items of clothing to the Chinese words
in the panel on the left. Test yourself using the cover flap.

1 衬衫
  chenshan

2 领带
  lingdai

3 袖子
  xiuzi

4 夹克衫
  jiakeshan

5 衣袋
  yidai

6 裤子
  kuzi

7 裙子
  qunzi

8 裤袜
  kuwa

9 鞋子
  xiezi

*shirt* ❶

*tie* ❷

*sleeve* ❸

*jacket* ❹

*pocket* ❺

*trousers* ❻

**Cultural tip** China has different
systems of sizes. Often clothes sizes are given
in a combination of height (in metres)
and chest size, or by using the
general size indicators (XL, L, M, S,
XS, etc.). Even allowing for
conversion of sizes, Chinese
clothes, and especially
shoes, tend to be smaller
than their Western
equivalents.

## 3 Useful phrases

Learn these phrases and then test yourself using the cover flap.

*Do you have a larger size?*

有大一号的吗？
you da yihao de ma

*It's not what I want.*

这不是我想要的
zhe bu shi wo xiang yao de

*I'll take the pink one.*

我要粉红色的
wo yao fenhong se de

## 4 Words to remember

Colours are adjectives (see p.64). Below, you will see the pure form of the colours, but often the character 色 **se** and/or 的 **de** is added depending on the sentence.

| | | |
|---|---|---|
| *red/pink* | 红/ 粉红 | hong/ fenhong |
| *white* | 白 | bai |
| *blue* | 蓝 | lan |
| *yellow* | 黄 | huang |
| *green* | 绿 | lv |
| *black* | 黑 | hei |

**7** *skirt*

**8** *tights*

**9** *shoes*

**Read it** The characters for colours are worth recognizing and they can often be seen in combination: 白酒 "baijui" white liquor; 红茶 "hongcha" red tea; 黄油 "huang-you" butter ("yellow fat"), 蓝图 "lantu" blueprint ("blue picture").

# Fuxi yu lianxi
## *Review and repeat*

## 1 Electronic

1 鼠标
shubiao

2 适配器
shipeiqi

3 变压器
bianyaqi

4 屏幕
pingmu

5 电池
dianchi

6 内存
neicun

7 保修证
baoxiuzheng

8 笔记本电脑
bijiben diannao

## 1 Electronic

Name the numbered items in Chinese.

❶ mouse
transformer ❸
adapter ❷
screen ❹
memory ❻
❺ battery  ❼ guarantee  ❽ laptop

## 2 Description

1 *That camera is too expensive.*

2 *My room is very noisy.*

3 *Do you have a larger size?*

## 2 Description

What do these phrases mean?

1 zhe jia xiangji tai gui

2 wo-de fangjian hen chaonao

3 you da yihao de ma

## 3 Shops

1 面包类
mianbaolei

2 熟食类
shushilei

3 蔬菜类
shucailei

4 鱼类
yulei

5 糕点类
gaodianlei

6 肉类
roulei

## 3 Shops

Name the numbered shops in Chinese. Then check your answers.

❶ baker  ❷ delicatessen  ❸ greengrocer

❹ fishmonger  ❺ cake shop  ❻ butcher

### 4 Supermarket

What is the Chinese for the numbered product categories?

❶ *drinks*

❷ *household products*

❸ *beauty products*

❹ *frozen foods*

❺ *snacks*

### 4 Supermarket

1 饮料
   yinliao

2 家庭用品
   jiatingyongpin

3 化妆品
   huazhuangpin

4 冷冻食品
   lengdongshipin

5 小吃
   xiaochi

### 5 Museum

Join in this conversation replying in Chinese following the English prompts.

nihao
1 *I'd like to buy four tickets.*

zhe shi nin-de menpiao
2 *What time do you close?*

women liudian zhong guanmen
3 *Is there a guidebook?*

you. daoyou ce mianfei
4 *Where's the lift?*

na bian you dianti
5 *Thank you.*

### 5 Museum

1 我要买四张门票。
   wo yao mai si zhang menpiao

2 你们什么时间关门？
   nimen shenme shijian guanmen

3 有导游册吗？
   you daoyou ce ma

4 电梯在哪里？
   dianti zai nali

5 谢谢你。
   xiexie ni

## 1 Warm up

Say "Han Hong is a student" and "I'm English." (pp.14–15)

Say "The internet café is in the centre of town." (pp.48–9)

# Gongzuo
## *Jobs*

Many Chinese words that are used to refer to occupations have the character 师 **shi** (*"master"*) or 生 **sheng** (*"person"*) at the end. The leader or head of a unit is indicated by the character 长 **zhang**. Businesses often have a tight hierarchy (see Cultural tip on p.79).

## 2 Words to remember: jobs

Familiarize yourself with these Chinese words and test yourself using the flap.

| | |
|---|---|
| 医生<br>yisheng | *doctor* |
| 牙医<br>yayi | *dentist* |
| 护士<br>hushi | *nurse* |
| 老师<br>laoshi | *teacher* |
| 会计师<br>kuaijishi | *accountant* |
| 律师<br>lvshi | *lawyer* |
| 设计师<br>shejishi | *designer* |
| 秘书<br>mishu | *secretary* |
| 店主<br>dianzhu | *shopkeeper* |
| 工程师<br>gongchengshi | *engineer* |
| 管道工<br>guandaogong | *plumber* |
| 厨师<br>chushi | *cook* |
| 个体户<br>getihu | *self-employed* |
| 学生<br>xuesheng | *student* |

我是商人。
wo shi shangren
*I'm a businessperson.*

我是会计师。
wo shi kuaijishi
*I'm an accountant.*

## 3 Put into practice

Join in this conversation. Use the cover flap to conceal the text on the right and complete the dialogue in Chinese.

您做什么工作?
**nin zuo shenme gongzuo**
*What's your profession?*

Say: *I'm a designer.*

我是设计师。
wo shi shejishi

您在哪个公司工作?
**nin zai na ge gongsi gongzuo**
*What company do you work for?*

Say: *I'm self-employed.*

我是个体户。
wo shi getihu

哦，是这样。
**o, shi zheyang**
*Oh, I see.*

Ask: *What's your profession?*

您做什么工作?
nin zuo shenme gongzuo

**Cultural tip** There are different titles for "manager" depending on the level. The order of seniority is 总经理 **zongjingli** (MD), 部门总监 **bumen zongjian** (director), 处长 **chuzhang** (head of division), 科长 **kezhang** (head of unit), 组长 **zuzhang** (group leader). Look out for the titles on business cards.

## 4 Words to remember: workplace

Familiarize yourself with these words and test yourself.

总部在上海。
zongbu zai shanghai
*The head office is in Shanghai.*

| | |
|---|---|
| *head office* | 总部<br>zongbu |
| *branch* | 分支机构<br>fenzhi jigou |
| *department* | 部<br>bu |
| *office worker* | 办公人员<br>bangong renyuan |
| *manager* | 经理<br>jingli |

Practise different ways of introducing yourself in different situations (pp.8–9). Mention your name, occupation, and any other information you'd like to volunteer (pp.12–13, pp.14–15).

# Bangongshi
*The office*

Traditionally, most adult Chinese would have a **sizhang**, an official seal or stamp bearing their name in characters. You may still see these stamps on official government papers and high-level contracts, although they are no longer the necessity they once were.

### 2 Words to remember

Familiarize yourself with these words. Read them aloud several times and try to memorize them. Conceal the Chinese with the cover flap and test yourself.

| | |
|---|---|
| 计算机 jisuanji | computer |
| 鼠标 shubiao | mouse |
| 电子邮件 dianzi youjian | e-mail |
| 因特网 yintewang | internet |
| 密码 mima | password |
| 留言机 liuyanji | voicemail |
| 传真 chuanzhen | fax |
| 复印 fuyin | photocopy |
| 复印机 fuyinji | photocopier |
| 书 shu | book |
| 日志 rizhi | diary |
| 名片 mingpian | business card |
| 会议 huiyi | meeting |
| 研讨会 yantaohui | conference |
| 会议日程 huiyi richeng | agenda |

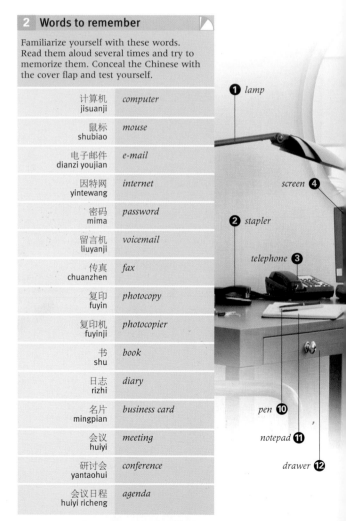

❶ lamp

❷ stapler

screen ❹

telephone ❸

pen ❿

notepad ⓫

drawer ⓬

## 3 Useful phrases

Learn these phrases and then test yourself using the cover flap.

| | | |
|---|---|---|
| | *I need to make some photocopies.* | 我需要复印资料。<br>wo xuyao fuyin ziliao |
| | *I'd like to arrange an appointment.* | 我想安排一次见面。<br>wo xiang anpai yici jianmian |
| | *I want to send an e-mail.* | 我要发送电子邮件。<br>wo yao fasong dianzi youjian |

## 4 Match and repeat

Match the numbered items to the Chinese words on the right.

**5** *keyboard*

**6** *laptop*

*printer* **9**

**7** *desk*

**8** *clock*

**13** *swivel chair*

1 灯
deng

2 订书机
dingshuji

3 电话
dianhua

4 屏幕
pingmu

5 键盘
jianpan

6 笔记本电脑
bijiben diannao

7 办公桌
bangongzhuo

8 闹钟
naozhong

9 打印机
dayinji

10 笔
bi

11 书写纸
shuxiezhi

12 抽屉
chouti

13 座椅
zuoyi

## 5 Say it

I'd like to arrange a meeting.

I want to send a fax.

Is there an agenda?

Say "Oh, I see!" (pp.78–9), "meeting" (pp.80–1), and appointment". (pp.32–3)

Ask "What's your profession?" and answer "I'm a lawyer." (pp.78–9)

# Zai yantaohui shang
## *At the conference*

University courses usually last four years and entrance to the top colleges is very competitive. High schools often start to prepare for the entrance exam many years in advance as future prospects can depend on which university a student attends. Once there, the pressure is less intense.

## 2 Useful phrases

Learn these phrases and then test yourself using the cover flap.

您是搞什么专业的?
nin shi gao shenme zhuanye de

*What's your field?*

我是搞研究的。
wo shi gao yanjiu de

*I'm doing research.*

我有法学学位。
wo you faxue xuewei

*I have a degree in law.*

我是建筑学讲师。
wo shi jianzhuxue jiangshi

*I'm a lecturer in architecture.*

## 3 In conversation

你好，我是严俊盟。
nihao, wo shi Yan Junmeng

*Hello, I'm Yan Junmeng.*

您在哪个大学任教?
nin zai na ge daxue renjiao

*Which university do you teach at?*

我在北京大学任教。
wo zai beijing daxue renjiao

*I teach at Beijing University.*

## 4 Words to remember

Familiarize yourself with these words and then test yourself.

| | |
|---|---|
| *conference (academic)* | 研讨会<br>yantaohui |
| *lecture* | 讲课<br>jiangke |
| *seminar* | 讲座<br>jiangzuo |
| *lecture theatre* | 教室<br>jiaoshi |
| *exhibition* | 展示会<br>zhanshihui |
| *university lecturer* | 大学讲师<br>daxuejiangshi |
| *professor* | 教授<br>jiaoshou |
| *medicine* | 医科<br>yi-ke |
| *science* | 理科<br>li-ke |
| *literature* | 文科<br>wen-ke |
| *engineering* | 工科<br>gong-ke |
| *law* | 法律<br>falv |
| *architecture* | 建筑学<br>jianzhuxue |
| *information technology* | "IT"<br>IT |

我们的展台在那边。
women-de zhantai zai nabian
*There's our exhibition stand.*

## 5 Say it

I teach at London University.

I have a degree in medicine.

I'm a lecturer in engineering.

您是搞什么专业的?
nin shi gao shenme zhuanye de

*What's your field?*

物理学。我也做研究。
wulixue. wo ye zuo yanjiu

*Physics. I'm also doing research.*

哦，是这样。
o, shi zheyang

*Oh, I see.*

Say "I want to send an e-mail." (pp.80–1)

Say "I'd like to arrange an appointment." (pp.80–1)

# Qiatan yewu
## *In business*

You will make a good impression if you make the effort to begin a meeting with a few words in Chinese, even if your vocabulary is limited. After that, all parties will probably be happy to continue in English. Remember to take business cards to exchange at meetings.

Familiarize yourself with these words and then test yourself by concealing the Chinese with the cover flap.

| | |
|---|---|
| 订单 dingdan | *order* |
| 交付 jiaofu | *delivery* |
| 付款 fukuan | *payment* |
| 预算 yusuan | *budget* |
| 价格 jiage | *price* |
| 文件 wenjian | *documents* |
| 发票 fapiao | *invoice* |
| 估算 gusuan | *estimate* |
| 利润 lirun | *profits* |
| 销售 xiaoshou | *sales* |
| 总计 zongji | *figures* |

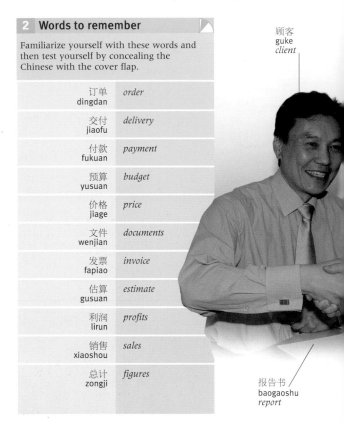

顾客
guke
*client*

报告书
baogaoshu
*report*

**Cultural tip** In general, business dealings are formal. However, the Chinese are famous for their hospitality. There's always an exchange of gifts at the end of a business meeting, so don't forget to bring something from home to show your appreciation.

## 3 Useful phrases

Practise these phrases. Note that the Chinese is necessarily very polite. It's better to err on the side of caution in a business context.

请给我看合同，好吗?
qing geiwo kan hetong,
hao ma
*Please show me
the contract.*

总经理
zongjingli
*managing
director*

请把合同送给我，好吗?
qing ba hetong song
geiwo, hao ma

*Can you send me the
contract, please?*

我们商定价格了吗?
women shangding
jiage le ma

*Have we agreed
a price?*

你们什么时候能交付?
nimen shenme shihou
neng jiaofu

*When can you make
the delivery?*

预算是多少?
yusuan shi duo shao

*How much is the
budget?*

### 4 Say it

Can you send me the invoice, please?

What's the price?

Please show me the order.

🇨🇳 **Read it** Some Chinese characters often re-occur in different combinations. Two of these are 机 **ji**, meaning "machine" or "device", and 电 **dian**, meaning "electric":

电话机 **dianhuaji** *telephone ("electric speaking machine")*

电脑 **diannao** *computer ("electric brain")*

电视机 **dianshiji** *television ("electric watching machine")*

复印机 **fuyinji** *photocopier ("copy machine")*

打印机 **diyanji** *printer ("printing machine")*

# Fuxi yu lianxi
*Review and repeat*

**Da an**
*Answers*
Cover with flap

## 1 At the office

1 灯
deng

2 笔记本电脑
bijiben diannao

3 笔
bi

4 订书机
dingshuji

5 办公桌
bangongzhuo

6 书写纸
shuxiezhi

7 闹钟
naozhong

## 1 At the office

Name these items in Chinese.

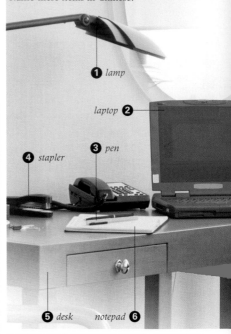

1 *lamp*

*laptop* 2

4 *stapler*    3 *pen*

5 *desk*    *notepad* 6

## 2 Jobs

1 医生
yisheng

2 管道工
guandaogong

3 店主
dianzhu

4 会计师
kuaijishi

5 学生
xuesheng

6 律师
lvshi

## 2 Jobs

What are these jobs in Chinese?

1 *doctor*

2 *plumber*

3 *shopkeeper*

4 *accountant*

5 *student*

6 *lawyer*

**Da an**
*Answers*
Cover with flap

## 3 Work

Answer these questions following the English prompts.

clock ❼

nin zuo shenme gongzuo
1 *Say "I'm a dentist."*

nin zai na ge gongsi gongzuo
2 *Say "I'm self-employed."*

nin zai na ge daxue renjiao
3 *Say "I teach at Beijing University."*

wei, wo shi zongji
4 *Say "I'd like to arrange an appointment."*

## 3 Work

1 我是牙医。
  wo shi yayi

2 我是个体户。
  wo shi getihu

3 我在北京大学任教。
  wo zai beijing daxue renjiao

4 我想安排一次见面。
  wo xiang anpai yici jianmian

## 4 How much?

Answer the question with the price shown in brackets.

1 kafei duo shao qian
  (¥30)

2 fangjian duo shao qian
  (¥800)

3 diannao duo shao qian
  (¥10,000)

4 chepiao duo shao qian
  (¥70)

## 4 How much?

1 三十元
  sanshi yuan

2 八百元
  babai yuan

3 一万元
  yiwan yuan

4 七十元
  qishi yuan

### 1 Warm up

Say "Can you give me the receipt?"
(pp.68–9)

Ask "Do you have any cakes?" (pp.18–19)

# Zai yaofang
## *At the chemist*

You may be asked **nali bu shufu** *(what's the matter?)*. To describe an ailment you can use the phrase **wo ... teng** *(I have a ... ache)*: **wo tou teng** *(I have a headache)*; **wo wei teng** *(I have a stomachache)*. Notice that the ailment or part of the body appears in the middle of the sentence.

### 2 Match and repeat

Match the numbered items to the Chinese words in the panel on the left and test yourself using the cover flap.

1 绷带
  bengdai

2 糖浆
  tangjiang

3 药水
  yaoshui

4 创可贴
  chuangketie

5 注射器
  zhusheqi

6 药片
  yaopian

7 栓剂
  shuanji

8 药膏
  yaogao

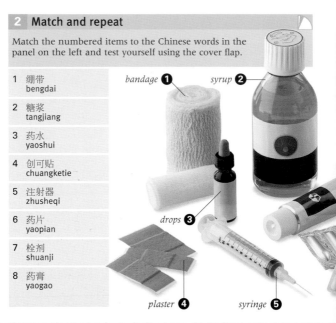

*bandage* ❶  *syrup* ❷

*drops* ❸

*plaster* ❹  *syringe* ❺

### 3 In conversation

你好，哪里不舒服?
nihao, nali bu shufu

*Hello. What's the matter?*

我胃痛。
wo wei teng

*I have a stomachache.*

你拉肚子吗?
ni laduzi ma

*Do you also have diarrhoea?*

### 4 Words to remember

Familiarize yourself with these words and test yourself using the flap.

| | | |
|---|---|---|
| *headache* | 头痛 | tou teng |
| *stomachache* | 胃痛 | wei teng |
| *diarrhoea* | 拉肚子 | laduzi |
| *cold* | 感冒 | ganmao |
| *cough* | 咳嗽 | kesou |
| *temperature* | 发烧 | fashao |
| *toothache* | 牙痛 | ya teng |

我头痛。
wo tou teng
*I have a headache.*

### 6 Say it

I have a toothache.

I have a cough.

Do you you have that as an ointment?

**8** *ointment*

**7** *suppository*

**6** *tablets*

### 5 Useful phrases

Learn these phrases and then test yourself using the cover flap.

| | | |
|---|---|---|
| *I have a leg ache.* | 我腿痛。 | wo tui teng |
| *Do you have that as a syrup?* | 这种药有糖浆型吗? | zhe zhong yao you tangjiang xing ma |
| *I'm allergic to penicillin.* | 我对青霉素过敏。 | wo dui qingmeisu guomin |

我不拉肚子，但是头痛。
wo bu laduzi, danshi tou teng

*No I don't, but I have a headache.*

吃这种药。
chi zhe zhong yao

*Take this.*

这种药有药片型吗?
zhe zhong yao you yaopian xing ma

*Do you have that as tablets?*

### 1 Warm up

Say " I have a toothache" and "I have leg ache." (pp.88–9)

Ask "What's the matter?" (pp.88–9)

# Shenti buwei
## *The body*

Most parts of the body have more than one word used to refer to them in Chinese. For example, **shoubi** *(arm)* is also called **gebo**, and **fu** *(stomach)* is also called **duz**. The words below are universally understood. Remember there is no plural, so **yan** is *eye* or *eyes* and **jiao** is *foot* or *feet*.

## 2 Match and repeat: body

Match the numbered parts of the body with the list on the left. Test yourself by using the cover flap.

1 手
shou

2 头
tou

3 肩膀
jianbang

4 肘
zhou

5 头发
toufa

6 手臂
shoubi

7 脖子
bozi

8 胸
xiong

9 腹
fu

10 腿
tui

11 膝
xi

12 脚
jiao

hand ❶

head ❷

shoulder ❸

❹ elbow

❺ hair

❻ arm

❼ neck

❽ chest

❾ stomach

❿ leg

⓫ knee

⓬ foot

## 3 Match and repeat: face

Match the numbered facial features with the list on the right.

*eye* ❶

❷ *eyebrow*

❸ *nose*

❹ *ear*

❺ *mouth*

| 1 | 眼 |
| | yan |
| 2 | 眉 |
| | mei |
| 3 | 鼻子 |
| | bizi |
| 4 | 耳朵 |
| | erduo |
| 5 | 嘴 |
| | zui |

## 4 Useful phrases

Learn these phrases and then test yourself using the cover flap.

*I have backache.*

我背痛。
wo bei teng

*I have a rash on my arm.*

我手臂上有疹子。
wo shoubi shang you zhenzi

*I don't feel well.*

我感觉不舒服。
wo ganjue bushufu

## 5 Put into practice

Join in this conversation and test yourself using the cover flap.

哪里不舒服?
nali bu shufu
*What's the matter?*

Say: I don't feel well.

我感觉不舒服。
wo ganjue bushufu

哪里痛?
nali teng
*Where does it hurt?*

Say: I have an ache in my shoulder.

我肩膀痛。
wo jianbang teng

## 1 Warm up

Say "I have a headache." (pp.88–9)

Now, say "I have an earache." (pp.90–1)

Ask "What's the matter?" (pp.88–9)

# Kan yisheng
*With the doctor*

Most Chinese doctors are based in hospitals rather than in separate clinics. You will usually need to go to a hospital for an appointment, even for minor ailments. Many Chinese doctors speak good English, but you could need to give a basic explanation in Chinese, for example, to a receptionist.

## 2 Useful phrases you may hear

Learn these phrases and then test yourself using the cover flap to conceal the Chinese on the left.

| | |
|---|---|
| 不严重。<br>bu yanzhong | *It's not serious.* |
| 需要化验。<br>xuyao huayan | *Tests are needed.* |
| 你骨折了。<br>ni guzhe le | *You have a fracture.* |
| 你需要住院。<br>ni xuyao zhuyuan | *You need to stay in hospital.* |

你是不是在服药?
ni shibushi zai fuyao
*Are you taking any medication?*

## 3 In conversation

哪里不舒服?
nali bu shufu

*What's the matter?*

我胸痛。
wo xiong teng

*I have a pain in my chest.*

让我听听。
rang wo tingting

*I'll need to examine you.*

### 4  Useful phrases you may need to say

Learn these phrases and then test yourself using the cover flap.

我怀孕了。
wo huaiyun le
*I'm pregnant.*

| | |
|---|---|
| *I have diabetes.* | 我有糖尿病。<br>wo you tangniaobing |
| *I have epilepsy.* | 我有癫痫症。<br>wo you dianxianzheng |
| *I have asthma.* | 我有哮喘病。<br>wo you xiaochuanbing |
| *I have a heart condition.* | 我有心脏病。<br>wo you xinzangbing |
| *I have a fever.* | 我发烧了。<br>wo fashao le |
| *It's urgent.* | 我要看急诊。<br>wo yao kan jizhen |
| *I feel breathless.* | 我感觉呼吸困难。<br>wo ganjue huxi kunnan |

### 5  Say it

I have a pain in my arm.

Is it urgent?

严重吗?
yanzhong ma

*Is it serious?*

不严重。只是消化不良。
bu yanzhong, zhishi xiaohuabuliang

*It's not serious. You only have indigestion.*

噢，那我就放心了。
o, na wo jiu fangxin le

*Oh! What a relief.*

## 1 Warm up

Say "Where's the florist?" (pp.68–9)

Say "Tests are needed." (pp.92–3)

What is the Chinese for "mouth" and "head"? (pp.90–1)

# Zai yiyuan
## *In hospital*

It is useful to know a few basic Chinese phrases relating to hospitals for use in an emergency or in case you need to visit a friend or colleague in hospital. Chinese medical care is not always available to foreigners, so make sure you have adequate insurance.

## 2 Useful phrases

Familiarize yourself with these phrases. Conceal the Chinese with the cover flap and test yourself.

| | |
|---|---|
| 候诊室在哪里?<br>houzhenshi zai nali | *Where's the waiting room?* |
| 需要多久?<br>xuyao duojiu | *How long does it take?* |
| 疼吗?<br>teng ma | *Will it hurt?* |
| 请躺在床上。<br>qing tang zai chuang shang | *Please lie down on the bed.* |
| 六小时之内请不要吃东西。<br>liu xiaoshi zhinei qing bu yao chi dongxi | *Please do not eat anything for six hours.* |
| 头不要动。<br>tou bu yao dong | *Don't move your head.* |
| 张开嘴。<br>zhang kai zui | *Open your mouth.* |
| 需要验血。<br>xuyao yanxue | *A blood test is needed.* |

护士
hushi
*nurse*

你感觉好些吗?
ni ganjue haoxie ma
*Are you feeling better?*

探望时间是几点钟?
tanwang shijian shi jidianzhong
*What are the visiting hours?*

### 3 Words to remember

Memorize these words and test yourself using the cover flap.

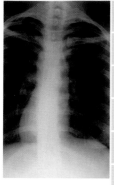

X光正常。
x-guang zhengchang
*The X-ray is normal.*

| | | |
|---|---|---|
| *emergency ward* | 急诊室 | jizhenshi |
| *children's ward* | 小儿病房 | xiaoer bingfang |
| *operating theatre* | 手术室 | shoushushi |
| *waiting room* | 候诊室 | houzhenshi |
| *corridor* | 走廊 | zoulang |
| *stairs* | 楼梯 | louti |
| *lift* | 电梯 | dianti |

### 4 Put into practice

Join in this conversation. Read the Chinese on the left and follow the instructions to make your reply. Then test yourself by hiding the answers with the cover flap.

不严重。
bu yanzhong
*It's not serious.*

Ask: Are tests needed?

需要化验吗?
xuyao huayan ma

需要验血。
xuyao yanxue
*A blood test is needed.*

Ask: Will it hurt?

疼吗?
teng ma

### 5 Say it

Is a blood test needed?

Where's the children's ward?

An X-ray is needed.

**Read it** The character for sickness is
病 **bing**. So 病房 **bingfang** ("sickness room")
is a ward, and 病人 **bingren** ("sick person")
is a patient. It's also useful to be able to
recognize the Chinese characters for
hospital. This literally means "medical
building": 医院 **yiyuan**.

# Fuxi yu lianxi
*Review and repeat*

## Da an
*Answers*
Cover with flap

## 1 The body

1 头
 tou

2 手臂
 shoubi

3 胸
 xiong

4 腹
 fu

5 腿
 tui

6 膝
 xi

7 脚
 jiao

## 1 The body

Name the numbered body parts in Chinese.

- **1** head
- **2** arm
- chest **3**
- **4** stomach
- leg **5**
- knee **6**
- foot **7**

## 2 On the phone

1 请给我接王先生的电话。
 qing geiwo jie Wang xiansheng de dianhua

2 我是大通印刷厂的杰克•亨特。
 wo shi datong yinshua chang de "Jieke Hengte"

3 我可以给他留言吗?
 wo keyi gei ta liuyan ma

4 会议不是星期四。
 huiyi bu shi xingqisi

5 谢谢你。
 xiexie ni

## 2 On the phone

You are arranging an appointment. Follow the conversation, replying in Chinese following the English prompts.

wei, wo shi zongji
1 *I'd like to speak to Mr Wang.*

nin shi shei ya
2 *I'm Jack Hunt of Tatong Printing.*

duibuqi, dianhua zhanxian
3 *Can I leave a message?*

dangran
4 *The meeting isn't on Tuesday.*

henhao
5 *Thank you.*

## 3 Clothing

Say the Chinese words for the numbered items of clothing.

jacket **1**

tie **2**

trousers **3**

shoes **4**

tights **5**

**6** skirt

### 3 Clothing

1 夹克衫
jiakeshan

2 领带
lingdai

3 裤子
kuzi

4 鞋
xiezi

5 裤袜
kuwa

6 裙子
qunzi

## 4 At the doctor's

Say these phrases in Chinese.

1 *I have a pain in my leg.*

2 *Is it serious?*

3 *I have a heart condition.*

4 *Will it hurt?*

5 *I'm pregnant.*

### 4 At the doctor's

1 我腿痛。
wo tui teng

2 严重吗?
yanzhong ma

3 我有心脏病。
wo you
xinzangbing

4 疼吗?
teng ma

5 我怀孕了。
wo huaiyun le

## 1 Warm up

Say the months of the year in Chinese. (pp.28–9)

Ask "Is there a museum nearby?" (pp.48–9) and "How much is that?" (pp.18–19)

# Jia li
## *Home*

In the bigger Chinese cities, space is limited and most urban Chinese traditionally live in apartments (**gongyu**). More recently, however, affluent suburbs have sprung up on the outskirts accommodating successful entrepreneurs and business owners in large houses and Western-style estates.

## 2 Match and repeat

Match the numbered items to the list and test yourself using the flap.

1 天沟
tiangou

2 阳台
yangtai

3 窗户
chuanghu

4 雨帘
yulian

5 屋顶
wuding

6 墙
qiang

7 门
men

8 台阶
taijie

9 花园
huayuan

❶ *gutter*  ❷ *balcony*  *window* ❸

*garden* ❾   *steps* ❽   *door* ❼

---

**Cultural tip** Features of buildings in China vary depending on the area, the climate, and the building materials available. In the north, heating is important, whereas in central and southern provinces, air-conditioning is a must. One almost universal feature is the presence of mosquito nets fixed on doors (**shamen**) and windows (**shachuang**).

## 3 Words to remember

Familiarize yourself with these words and test yourself using the flap.

| | | |
|---|---|---|
| *room* | 房间 | fangjian |
| *floor* | 地板 | diban |
| *ceiling* | 天花板 | tianhuaban |
| *bedroom* | 卧室 | woshi |
| *bathroom* | 卫生间 | weishengjian |
| *kitchen* | 厨房 | chufang |
| *dining room* | 餐厅 | canting |
| *living room* | 客厅 | keting |
| *attic* | 阁楼 | gelou |
| *parking space* | 车库 | cheku |

房租每月多少钱?
fangzu mei yue duo
shao qian
*How much is the rent
per month?*

4 canopy    5 roof

6 wall

## 4 Useful phrases

Learn these phrases and test yourself.

有车库吗?
you cheku ma

*Is there a parking
space?*

我什么时候能搬进
来?
wo shenme shihou
neng ban jinlai

*When can I move in?*

家具齐全吗?
jiaju qiquan ma

*Is it furnished?*

## 5 Say it

Is there a dining
room?

Where's the kitchen?

It's furnished.

## 1 Warm up

What's the Chinese for "table" (pp.20–1), "desk" (pp.80–1), "bed" (pp.60–1), and "curtains"? (pp.60–1)

How do you say "This car is small"? (pp.64–5)

# Wu nei
## *Inside the home*

The Chinese often end their sentences with short "markers" that don't really change the meaning but carry different nuances. For example, the **yo** marker can imply *"and even"* or *"to be sure"* and **ne** can mean something like *"isn't that so?"* You'll see examples of these in the conversation below.

## 2 Match and repeat

Match the numbered items to the list in the panel on the left. Then test yourself by concealing the Chinese with the cover flap.

1 水池
  shuichi

2 水龙头
  shuilongtou

3 电饭煲
  dianfanbao

4 厨台
  chutai

5 洗碗机
  xiwanji

6 椅子
  yizi

7 柜橱
  guichu

8 桌子
  zhuozi

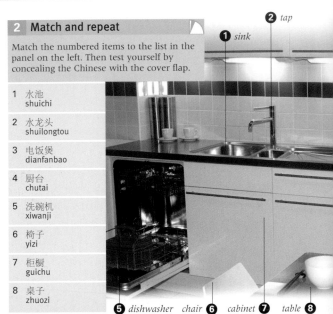

❶ *sink*  ❷ *tap*

❺ *dishwasher*  *chair* ❻  *cabinet* ❼  *table* ❽

## 3 In conversation

这是冰箱。
zhe shi bingxiang

*This is the fridge.*

有电饭煲吗?
you dianfanbao ma

*Is there a rice cooker?*

有。那是炉灶。
you. na shi luzao

*Yes, there is. And here's the stove.*

### 4  Words to remember

Familiarize yourself with these words and test yourself using the flap.

沙发是新的呢。
shafa shi xin de ne
*This sofa is new.*

| | | |
|---|---|---|
| *sofa* | 沙发 | shafa |
| *carpet* | 地毯 | ditan |
| *bath* | 浴缸 | yugang |
| *toilet* | 洗手间 | xishoujian |
| *stove* | 炉灶 | luzao |
| *washing machine* | 洗衣机 | xiyiji |
| *fridge* | 冰箱 | bingxiang |

**3** *rice cooker*

*worktop* **4**

### 5  Useful phrases

Learn these phrases and then test yourself using the cover flap to conceal the Chinese.

| | | |
|---|---|---|
| *I'm not fond of the curtains.* | 我不喜欢这种窗帘。 | wo bu xihuan zhezhong chuanglian |
| *The fridge is broken.* | 冰箱坏了。 | bingxiang huai le |
| *Are heat and electricity included?* | 包含供暖和供电吗? | baohan gongnuan he gongdian ma |

### 6  Say it

Is there a washing machine?

The fridge is new.

The tap is broken.

水池是新的呢。
shuichi shi xin de ne

*The sink is new.*

还有洗碗机呢。
haiyou xiwanji ne

*And there's even a dishwasher.*

瓷砖真好看哟。
cizhuan zhenhao kan yo

*What pretty tiles!*

## 1 Warm up

What's the Chinese for "day" and "month"? (pp.28–9)

Say "Where's the florist?" (pp.68–9) and "Is there a garden?" (pp.98–9)

# Huayuan
## *The garden*

Chinese gardens, often with water features and plants like pine trees and bamboos, can be seen in public places such as parks, pagodas, and hotels. Space constraints mean that many Chinese homes don't have their own gardens, but house plants and flower arrangements are popular.

## 2 Words to remember

Familiarize yourself with these words and test yourself using the flap.

| | |
|---|---|
| 春<br>chun | spring |
| 夏<br>xia | summer |
| 秋<br>qiu | autumn |
| 冬<br>dong | winter |

pagoda ❶

tree ❷

stones ❿

pond ❾

rocks ❽

❼ plants

## 3 Useful phrases

Learn these phrases and then test yourself using the cover flap.

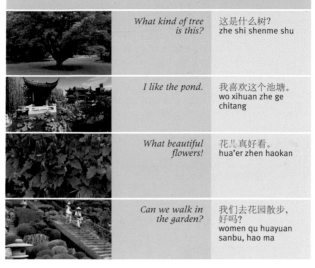

| | | |
|---|---|---|
| | *What kind of tree is this?* | 这是什么树?<br>zhe shi shenme shu |
| | *I like the pond.* | 我喜欢这个池塘。<br>wo xihuan zhe ge chitang |
| | *What beautiful flowers!* | 花儿真好看。<br>hua'er zhen haokan |
| | *Can we walk in the garden?* | 我们去花园散步,好吗?<br>women qu huayuan sanbu, hao ma |

## 4 Match and repeat

Match the numbered items to the words in the panel on the right.

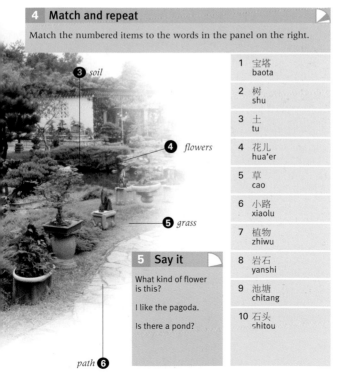

**3** soil

**4** flowers

**5** grass

path **6**

| | |
|---|---|
| 1 | 宝塔<br>baota |
| 2 | 树<br>shu |
| 3 | 土<br>tu |
| 4 | 花儿<br>hua'er |
| 5 | 草<br>cao |
| 6 | 小路<br>xiaolu |
| 7 | 植物<br>zhiwu |
| 8 | 岩石<br>yanshi |
| 9 | 池塘<br>chitang |
| 10 | 石头<br>shitou |

### 5 Say it

What kind of flower is this?

I like the pagoda.

Is there a pond?

## 1 Warm up

Say "My name is John." (pp.8–9)

Say "I like the pond." (pp.102–3)

What's "fish" in Chinese? (pp.22–3)

# Dongwu
## *Animals*

The Chinese tend to keep small dogs such as Pekinese and sometimes cats in the house as pets. Birds and fish are also very popular. Keeping pets is generally becoming more popular, although official licences are required, which can be expensive.

## 2 Match and repeat

Match the numbered animals to the Chinese words in the panel on the left. Then test yourself using the cover flap.

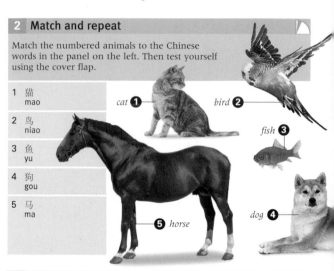

1 猫
  mao

2 鸟
  niao

3 鱼
  yu

4 狗
  gou

5 马
  ma

*cat* ❶

*bird* ❷

*fish* ❸

*dog* ❹

❺ *horse*

## 3 Useful phrases

Learn these phrases and then test yourself using the cover flap.

| | |
|---|---|
| 别担心，它很亲热人。<br>bie danxin, ta hen qinre ren | *Don't worry. He's friendly.* |
| 它叫什么名字?<br>ta jiao shenme mingzi | *What's his name?* |
| 我不喜欢猫。<br>wo bu xihuan mao | *I'm not fond of cats.* |
| 这狗不咬人。<br>zhe gou bu yao ren | *This dog doesn't bite.* |

这是你家的猫吗?
zhe shi ni jia de mao ma
*Is this your cat?*

**Cultural tip** Some buildings and big houses will keep larger dogs outside, as guard dogs. These are known for their toughness and are treated as "yard" dogs rather than as pets. Look out for the "Beware of the dog" (**xiaoxin you gou**) sign.

---

## 4 Words to remember

Familiarize yourself with these words and test yourself using the flap.

| | | |
|---|---|---|
| *monkey* | 猴 | hou |
| *sheep* | 羊 | yang |
| *cow* | 牛 | niu |
| *pig* | 猪 | zhu |
| *rabbit* | 兔 | tu |
| *tiger* | 虎 | hu |

这是什么鱼?
zhe shi shenme yu
*What kind of fish is this?*

**Read it** Most basic words referring to natural features or animals, such as "tree", "dog", "flower", "cow", etc., are written with just a single character. Look at the characters for animals and natural features in week 10 and see if you can spot them in the phrases.

---

## 5 Put into practice

Join in this conversation. Read the Chinese on the left and follow the instructions to make your reply. Then test yourself by concealing the answers with the cover flap.

这是你家的狗吗?
zhe shi ni jia de gou ma
*Is this your dog?*

Say: *Yes, his name is Guoguo.*

是的。它的名字叫果果。
shide. ta de mingzi jiao guoguo

我不喜欢狗。
wo bu xihuan gou
*I'm not fond of dogs.*

Say: *Don't worry. He's friendly.*

别担心, 它很亲热人。
bie danxin, ta hen qinre ren

# Fuxi yu lianxi
## *Review and repeat*

**Da an**
*Answers*
Cover with flap

### 1 Colours

1 白
bai

2 黄
huang

3 绿
lv

4 黑
hei

5 红
hong

6 蓝
lan

7 粉红
fenhong

### 1 Colours

What are these colours in Chinese?

1 *white*

2 *yellow*

3 *green*

4 *black*

5 *red*

6 *blue*

7 *pink*

### 2 Kitchen

1 厨台
chutai

2 水池
shuichi

3 水龙头
shuilongtou

4 电饭煲
dianfanbao

5 洗碗机
xiwanji

6 椅子
yizi

7 柜橱
guichu

8 桌子
zhuozi

### 2 Kitchen

Say the Chinese words for the numbered items.

❶ *worktop*   *sink* ❷   ❸ *tap*

*dishwasher* ❺   *chair* ❻   *cabinet* ❼

### 3 House

You are visiting a house in China. Join in the conversation, replying in Chinese where you see the English prompts.

zhe shi weishengjian
1 *What pretty tiles!*

zhe shi guanxishi
2 *Is there a washing machine?*

you xiyiji
3 *Is there a parking space?*

mei you cheku. you huayuan
4 *Is it furnished?*

jiaju qiquan
5 *How much is the rent per month?*

### 3 House

1 瓷砖真好看哟。
   cizhuan zhenhao
   kan yo

2 有洗衣机吗?
   you xiyiji ma

3 有车库吗?
   you cheku ma

4 家具齐全吗?
   jiaju qiquan ma

5 房租每月多少钱?
   fangzu mei yue
   duo shao qian

### 4 At home

Say the Chinese for the following items.

1 *washing machine*

2 *sofa*

3 *attic*

4 *dining room*

5 *tree*

6 *garden*

4 rice cooker

8 table

### 4 At home

1 洗衣机
   xiyiji

2 沙发
   shafa

3 阁楼
   gelou

4 餐厅
   canting

5 树
   shu

6 花园
   huayuan

# Youju he yinhang
*Post office and bank*

## 1 Warm up

Ask "How do I get to the station?", and "Where's the post office?" (pp.50–1 and pp.68–9)

What's the Chinese for "passport"? (pp.54–5)

Ask "What time is it?" (pp.30–1)

Post office signs or buildings and postboxes are painted green in China. Most banks are open for business on Sundays. Only the Bank of China handles currency exchange and their ATMs allow foreign bank cards to withdraw Chinese currency (**Renminbi**) up to certain limits.

## 2 Words to remember: post

Familiarize yourself with these words and test yourself using the cover flap to conceal the Chinese on the left.

| | |
|---|---|
| 邮局 youju | *post office* |
| 信件 xinjian | *letter* |
| 信封 xinfeng | *envelope* |
| 邮包 youbao | *parcel* |
| 航空邮件 hangkong youjian | *air mail* |
| 邮票 youpiao | *stamps* |
| 邮递员 youdiyuan | *postman* |
| 邮箱 youxiang | *postbox* |

明信片
mingxinpian
*postcard*

## 3 In conversation

请给我兑换旅行支票，好吗?
qing geiwo duihuan lvxingzhipiao, hao ma

*I'd like to change some traveller's cheques.*

您有身份证吗?
nin you shenfenzheng ma

*Do you have any identification?*

有。这是我的护照。
you. zhe shi wo-de huzhao

*Yes, I do. Here's my passport.*

## 4 Words to remember: bank

Familiarize yourself with these words and test yourself using the cover flap to conceal the Chinese on the right.

信用卡
xinyongka
*credit card*

我能用信用卡付款吗?
wo neng yong xinyongka
fukuan ma
*Can I pay with a credit
card?*

| | | |
|---|---|---|
| *bank* | 银行 | yinhang |
| *money* | 钱 | qian |
| *traveller's cheques* | 旅行支票 | lvxingzhipiao |
| *banknotes* | 纸币 | zhibi |
| *coins* | 硬币 | yingbi |
| *cash point* | 自动提款机 | zidong tikuanji |
| *exchange rate* | 汇率 | huilv |

## 5 Useful phrases

Learn these phrases and then test yourself using the cover flap.

## 6 Say it

I'd like to change
some dollars.

Here's my credit card.

Where's the postbox?

| | |
|---|---|
| *I'd like to change some money, please.* | 请给我换点钱，好吗? qing geiwo huandian qian, hao ma |
| *What is the exchange rate?* | 汇率是多少? huilv shi duoshao |
| *Where's the cash point?* | 哪里有自动提款机? nali you zidong tikuanji |

请在这里签字。
qing zai zheli qianzi

*Please sign here.*

您要多大面值的纸币?
nin yao duoda mianzhi
de zhibi

*How would you like
the notes?*

请给我100元面值的。
qing geiwo yibai yuan
mianzhi de

*I'd like 100-yuan
notes, please.*

## 1 Warm up

What is the Chinese for "The fridge is broken"? (pp.100–1)

What's the Chinese for "today" and "tomorrow"? (pp.28–9)

Say "Thank you." (pp. 40–1)

# Xiuli
## *Repairs*

You can combine the Chinese words on these pages with the vocabulary you learned in week 10 to help you explain basic problems and cope with arranging most repairs. Rented accommodation is usually arranged via agents, known as **zufang zhongjie**. They can also help with problems.

## 2 Words to remember

Familiarize yourself with these words and test yourself using the flap.

| 管道工 guandaogong | *plumber* |
| 电工 diangong | *electrician* |
| 机械师 jixieshi | *mechanic* |
| 修理工 xiuligong | *handyman* |
| 木匠 mujiang | *carpenter* |
| 电脑修理店 diannao xiulidian | *computer repair shop* |
| 清洁工 qingjiegong | *cleaner* |
| 厨师 chushi | *cook* |

我想请一名机械师。
wo xiang qing yiming jixieshi
*I need a mechanic.*

## 3 In conversation

早上好。我是韩红。
zaoshang hao. wo shi Han Hong

*Good morning. This is Han Hong.*

早上好。有什么问题吗?
zaoshang hao. you shenme wenti ma

*Good morning. Is there a problem?*

洗碗机坏了。
xiwanji huai le

*The dishwasher is broken.*

## 4 Useful phrases

Learn these phrases and then test yourself using the cover flap.

| | | |
|---|---|---|
| *Please clean the room.* | 请整理房间吧。 | qing zhengli fangjian ba |
| *Can you repair the television?* | 你能修理电视机吗? | ni neng xiuli dianshiji ma |
| *Can you recommend a good handyman?* | 你能推荐一个好的修理工吗? | ni neng tuijian yige hao de xiuligong ma |

哪里才能修理它呢?
nali caineng xiuli ta ne
*Where can I get this repaired?*

## 5 Put into practice

Cover up the text on the right and complete the dialogue in Chinese.

您的光驱坏了。
nin-de guangqu huai le
*Your CD drive is broken.*

*Ask: Can you recommend a good computer repair shop?*

你能推荐一个好的电脑修理店吗?
ni neng tuijian yige hao de diannao xiulidian ma

街上有一家。
jieshang you yijia
*There's one in the town.*

谢谢你。
xiexie ni

今天能修理。
jintian neng xiuli
*It's possible to repair it today.*

*Say: Thank you.*

我们会派一名修理工去。
women hui pai yiming xiuligong qu

*We'll send a handyman.*

今天就派, 好吗?
jintian jiu pai, hao ma

*Can you do it today, please?*

对不起。明天上午派。
duibuqi. mingtian shangwu pai

*Sorry. But it will be tomorrow morning.*

Say the days of the week in Chinese. (pp.28–9)

How do you say "cleaner"? (pp.110–11)

Say "It's 9.30", "10.45", and "12.00." (pp.30–1)

# Lai
## *To come*

Chinese verbs generally do not change with the subject (I, you, he, she, we, they). Sometimes, however, these verbs need to be followed by time-indicating characters. Below, you will see some of these changes for the verb 来 **lai** *(to come)*.

### 2 Useful phrases

Say the different forms of **lai** *(to come)* aloud. Use the cover flap to test yourself and, when you are confident, practise the sample sentences below.

| | |
|---|---|
| 来<br>lai | *to come*<br>*(infinitive)* |
| 来了<br>lai le | *come/coming*<br>*(present)* |
| 不来了<br>bu lai le | *not come/coming*<br>*(present negative)* |
| 来过<br>lai guo | *came*<br>*(past)* |
| 没来过<br>mei lai guo | *didn't come*<br>*(past negative)* |
| 来吧!<br>lai ba | *Please come!*<br>*(invitation)* |
| 公共汽车来了。<br>gonggongqiche lai le | *The bus is coming.* |
| 木匠9点钟来过<br>mujiang jiu dianzhong lai guo | *The carpenter came at nine o'clock.* |
| 清洁工今天没来过。<br>qingjiegong jintian mei lai guo | *The cleaner didn't come today.* |
| 我明天来。<br>wo mingtian lai | *I'll come tomorrow.* |

他们乘火车来。
tamen cheng huoche lai
*They're coming by train.*

**Conversational tip** Beware of English phrases using "come" that translate differently in Chinese. For example, the Chinese equivalent of "I come from Canada" would be "wo shi jianada ren", which translates literally as " I am Canada person".

## 3 Invitations

You can use **lai** (*come*) for invitations. There are different expressions depending on the level of formality.

请来参加我的生日晚会吧。
qing lai canjia wo-de shengri wanhui ba

*Please come to join my birthday party.*

星期一您能不能来我们的接待室?
xingqiyi nin nengbuneng lai women-de jiedaishi

*On Monday, can you come to our reception? (formal)*

星期五您能不能来参加我们的座谈会?
xingqiwu nin nengbuneng lai canjia women-de zuotanhui

*On Friday, can you come to join our seminar? (formal)*

来参加我的晚宴吧!
lai canjia wo-de wanyan ba

*Come to my dinner party! (informal)*

## 4 Put into practice

Join in this conversation. Read the Chinese on the left and follow the instructions to make your reply. Then test yourself by concealing the answers with the cover flap.

喂, 你好。
wei, nihao
*Hello.*

Say: *Hello. Please come to join my birthday party.*

你好。请来参加我的生日晚会吧。
nihao. qing lai canjia wo-de shengri wanhui ba

晚会什么时候开始?
wanhui shenme shihou kaishi
*What time does the party begin?*

Say: *Eight o'clock, tomorrow evening.*

明天晚上8点。
mingtian wanshang badian

好。我一定来。
hao. wo yiding lai
*Yes, I'd love to come.*

Say: *See you tomorrow.*

明天见。
mingtian jian

## 1 Warm up

What's the Chinese for "tall" and "short"? (pp.64–5)

Say "The room is big" and "The bed is small." (pp.64–5)

# Jingcha yu fanzui
## *Police and crime*

Chinese police cars have the two characters 公安 **gong-an** (*public security*) or 交警 **jiaojing** (*traffic police*) displayed. Note that the terms **nanren** (*man*) and **nvren** (*woman*) in section 4 are not very polite as they refer to criminal suspects. More polite equivalents would be **nanshi** and **nvshi**.

## 2 Words to remember: crime

Familiarize yourself with these words.

| | |
|---|---|
| 扒手 pashou | thief/burglar |
| 警方报告 jingfang baogao | police report |
| 证词 zhengci | statement |
| 证人 zhengren | witness |
| 目击者 mujizhe | eye-witness |
| 律师 lvshi | lawyer |
| 警官 jingguan | police officer |

我需要请律师。
wo xuyao qing lvshi
*I need a lawyer.*

## 3 Useful phrases

Learn these phrases and then test yourself using the cover flap.

| | |
|---|---|
| 我的手袋被偷了。 wo shoudai bei tou le | I've been pick-pocketed. |
| 丢失了什么? diushi le shenme | What was stolen? |
| 你看见是谁偷的吗? ni kanjian shi shei tou de ma | Did you see who did it? |
| 什么时候发生的? shenme shihou fa sheng de | When did it happen? |

照相机
zhaoxiangji
*camera*

钱
qian
*money*

钱包
qianbao
*wallet*

## 4 Words to remember: appearance

Learn these words and then test yourself using the cover flap.

那男人棕色头发，戴眼镜。
na nanren zongse toufa, daiyanjing
*The man had brown hair and glasses.*

那女人很高，长头发。
na nvren hen gao, chang toufa
*The woman was tall and had long hair.*

| | | |
|---|---|---|
| *man/men* | 男人 | nanren |
| *woman/women* | 女人 | nvren |
| *tall* | 高 | gao |
| *short* | 矮 | ai |
| *young* | 青年 | qingnian |
| *middle-aged* | 中年 | zhongnian |
| *fat* | 胖 | pang |
| *thin* | 瘦 | shou |
| *with a beard* | 有落腮胡子 | you luosaihuzi |
| *with a moustache* | 有小胡子 | you xiaohuzi |
| *wearing glasses* | 戴眼镜 | daiyanjing |

> **Read it** The Chinese for "police" is written with two characters: 警察 (jingcha). Changing the last of these characters to 官 (guan) will produce "police officer": 警官 (jingguan); and adding the character 局 (ju) will produce the word for "police station": 警察局 (jingchaju).

## 5 Put into practice

Practise these phrases. Then use the cover flap to hide the text on the right and follow the instructions to make your reply in Chinese.

他长得什么样?
ta zhangde shenme yang
*Can you describe him?*

Say: *The man was short.*

那男人很矮。
na nanren hen ai

头发呢?
toufa ne
*And the hair?*

Say: *Brown hair with a beard.*

棕色头发，有落腮胡子。
zangse toufa, you luosaihuzi

# Fuxi yu lianxi
*Review and repeat*

## 1 To come

1 我乘公共汽车来。
wo cheng
gonggong qiche lai

2 昨天电工来过。
zuotian diangong
lai guo

3 请来参加我的生
日晚会。
qing lai canjia wo-
de shengri wanhui

4 星期四清洁工没
来过。
xingqisi
qingjiegong mei
lai guo

## 1 To come

Put the following sentences into Chinese
using the correct form of **lai** (*to come*).

1 *I'm coming by bus.*

2 *The electrician came yesterday.*

3 *Please come and join my birthday party.*

4 *The cleaner didn't come on Thursday.*

## 2 Bank and post

1 信用卡
xinyongka

2 纸币
zhibi

3 明信片
mingxinpian

4 信封
xinfeng

5 邮票
youpiao

## 2 Bank and post

Name the numbered
items in Chinese.

credit card **1**

banknotes **2**

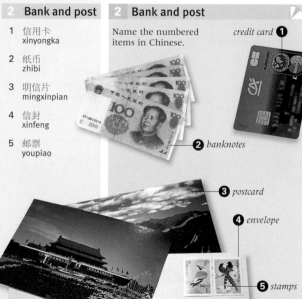

postcard **3**

envelope **4**

stamps **5**

## 3 Appearance

What do these descriptions mean?

1 ta shi aigezi, yeshi shouzi

2 na nanren you duantoufa

3 na nvren daiyanjing

4 na nanren you xiaohuzi

5 ta toufa huabai, you luosaihuzi

## 4 The pharmacy

You are asking a pharmacist for advice. Join in the conversation, replying in Chinese where you see the English prompts.

nihao, nali bu shufu
1 *I have a stomachache.*

ni laduzi ma
2 *No, but I have a headache.*

chi zhe zhong yao
3 *Do you have that as a syrup?*

you
4 *How much is that?*

wushi yuan
5 *Thank you.*

## Da an
*Answers*
Cover with flap

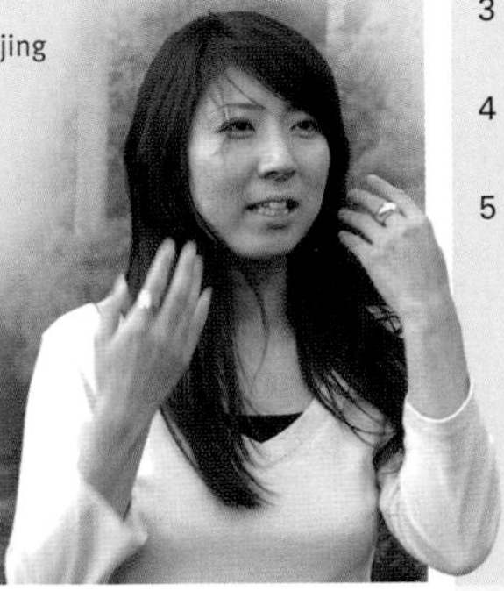

### 3 Appearance

1 *He/She was short and thin.*

2 *The man had short hair.*

3 *The woman wears glasses.*

4 *The man had a moustache.*

5 *He had grey hair with a beard.*

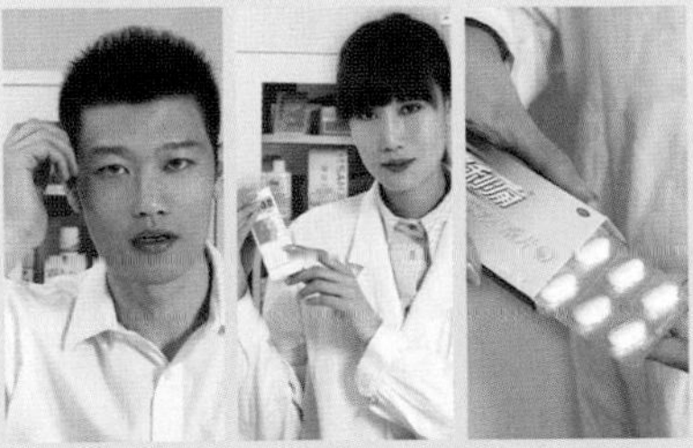

### 4 The pharmacy

1 我胃痛。
wo wei teng

2 不。我头痛
bu. wo tou teng

3 这种药有糖浆型吗?
zhe zhong yao you tangjiang xing ma

4 多少钱?
duo shao qian

5 谢谢。
xiexie

## 1 Warm up

What is the Chinese for "museum" and "cinema?" (pp.48–9)

Say "I like the pond." (pp.102–3)

Ask "What's your profession?" (pp.78–9)

# Xiuxian yule
## *Leisure time*

Popular leisure activities outside the house include shopping and going to karaoke bars, and going to the cinema. **Pu-ke** *(cards)*, **ma-jiang** *(mahjong)*, **xiang-qi** *(Chinese chess)*, and other traditional games are popular with older people, while theatre and opera are only minority pursuits.

## 2 Words to remember

Familiarize yourself with these words and test yourself using the cover flap to conceal the Chinese on the left.

我喜欢看京剧。
wo xihuan kan jingju
*I like Chinese opera.*

演员
yanyuan
*actor*

| | |
|---|---|
| 剧场<br>juchang | *theatre* |
| 看电影<br>kandianying | *watching films* |
| 主题公园<br>zhutigongyuan | *theme park* |
| 音乐<br>yinyue | *music* |
| 艺术<br>yishu | *art* |
| 体育<br>tiyu | *sport* |
| 旅游<br>lvyou | *travelling* |
| 读书<br>dushu | *reading* |

## 3 In conversation

你想去卡拉OK厅吗?
ni xiang qu kala-ok ting ma

*Do you want to go to a karaoke bar?*

我并不喜欢卡拉OK。
wo bing bu xihuan kala-ok

*I don't really like karaoke.*

你业余时间做什么?
ni yeyushijian zuo shenme

*What do you do in your free time?*

## 4 Useful phrases

Learn these phrases and then test yourself using the cover flap.

| | |
|---|---|
| *What do you do in your free time? (formal)* | 您业余时间做什么?<br>nin yeyushijian zuo shenme |
| *What do you do in your free time? (informal).* | 你业余时间做什么?<br>ni yeyushijian zuo shenme |
| *My hobby is reading.* | 我的爱好是读书。<br>wo-de aihao shi dushu |
| *I like watching films.* | 我喜欢看电影。<br>wo xihuan kandianying |
| *I hate shopping.* | 我最不喜欢购物了。<br>wo zui bu xihuan gouwu le |

我喜欢玩电子游戏。
wo xihuan wan dianzi youxi
*I like video games.*

布景
bujing
*set*

舞台
wutai
*stage*

## 5 Say it

I like music.

I don't really like watching films.

My hobby is opera.

I hate theme parks.

我喜欢购物。
wo xihuan gouwu

*I like shopping.*

我最不喜欢购物了。
wo zui bu xihuan gouwu le

*I hate shopping.*

没问题。我自己去。
mei wenti. wo ziji qu

*No problem, I'll go on my own.*

### 1 Warm up

What's the Chinese for "fish"? (pp.104–5)

Say "I like the theatre" and "I like travelling." (pp.118–9)

Say "I don't really like..." (pp.118–9)

# Tiyu yu aihao
## *Sport and hobbies*

Traditional Chinese sports, which are still popular, include martial arts **xiangqi**, Chinese wrestling **weiqi(go)**, and dragon-boat racing. Basketball, table tennis, badminton, football, and golf have also established themselves. Arts and crafts include embroidery, paper-cutting, and calligraphy.

### 2 Words to remember

Memorize these words and then test yourself.

| | |
|---|---|
| 足球 zuqiu | *football* |
| 篮球 lanqiu | *basketball* |
| 乒乓 pingpang | *table tennis* |
| 游泳 youyong | *swimming* |
| 登山 dengshan | *mountain climbing* |
| 钓鱼 diaoyu | *fishing* |
| 画画 huahua | *painting* |
| 书法 shufa | *calligraphy* |

沙坑 shakeng *bunker*

高尔夫球手 gao-er-fu qiushou *golfer*

我每天打高尔夫。 wo meitian da gao-er-fu *I play golf every day.*

### 3 Useful phrases

Familiarize yourself with these phrases.

| | |
|---|---|
| 我打球 wo da bangqiu | *I play baseball.* |
| 他打乒乓。 ta da pingpang | *He plays table tennis.* |
| 她喜欢画画。 ta xihuan huahua | *She likes painting.* |

## 4 Phrases to remember

Learn the phrases below and then test yourself. Notice that "play" is **da** or **ti** (literally "kick") for sports, but **la** for musical instruments.

| | |
|---|---|
| *What do you like doing? (formal)* | 您想做什么? nin xiang zuo shenme |
| *What do you like doing? (informal)* | 你想玩儿什么? ni xiang wan'er shenme |
| *I like playing golf.* | 我想打高尔夫。 wo xiang da gao-er-fu |
| *I like playing table tennis.* | 我想打乒乓。 wo xiang da pingpang |
| *I play football.* | 我踢足球。 wo ti zuqiu |
| *I like going fishing.* | 我想去钓鱼。 wo xiang qu diaoyu |
| *I go mountain climbing.* | 我去登山。 wo qu dengshan |

我拉小提琴。
wo la xiaotiqin
*I play the violin.*

旗子
qizi
*flag*

高尔夫球场
gao-er-fu qiuchang
*golf course*

## 5 Put into practice

Learn these phrases. Then cover up the text on the right and complete the dialogue in Chinese. Check your answers.

| | |
|---|---|
| 你想玩儿什么? ni xiang wan'er shenme *What do you like doing?* <br><br> *Say: I like playing football.* | 我想踢足球。 wo xiang ti zuqiu |
| 你打篮球吗? ni da lanqiu ma *Do you play basketball?* <br><br> *Say: No, I play golf.* | 不。我打高尔夫。 bu. wo da gao-er-fu |
| 你经常打吗? ni jingchang da ma *Do you play often?* <br><br> *Say: Every week.* | 每星期打一次。 meixingqi da yici |

## 1 Warm up

Say "your husband" and "your wife." (pp.12–13)

How do you say "lunch" and "dinner" in Chinese? (pp.20–1)

Say "Sorry, I'm busy that day." (pp.32–3)

# Shejiao
## *Socializing*

As a business guest, it's more common to be invited to a restaurant than to someone's home. This is partly practical – people often have long commutes. But if you're staying for longer, you may be invited for a meal or a party.

## 2 Useful phrases

Learn these phrases and then test yourself.

| | |
|---|---|
| 您想来参加晚宴吗? <br> nín xiang lai canjia wanyan ma | *Would you like to come for dinner?* |
| 星期三怎么样? <br> xingqisan zenmeyang | *What about Wednesday?* |
| 下一次吧。 <br> xiayici ba | *Perhaps another time.* |

**Cultural tip** When visiting a Chinese home, remember that it's usual to remove your outdoor shoes at the door. Take a gift for the host or hostess. Flowers, a bottle of drink, or a present from your home country will be greatly appreciated.

## 3 In conversation

您想来参加星期二的晚宴吗?
nín xiang lai canjia xingqi'er de wanyan ma

*Would you like to come for dinner on Tuesday?*

对不起，我星期二很忙。
duibuqi, wo xingqi'er henmang

*Sorry. I'm busy on Tuesday.*

星期四怎么样?
xingqisi zenmeyang

*What about Thursday?*

## 4 Words to remember

Familiarize yourself with these words and test yourself using the flap.

客人
keren
*guest*

东道主
dongdaozhu
*host*

| | | |
|---|---|---|
| *party* | 晚会 | wanhui |
| *invitation* | 邀请 | yaoqing |
| *gift* | 礼物 | liwu |

**Read it** You now know the principle of how the Chinese script works and can recognize some basic recurring characters. You'll also find more information on pp.152–7 to further expand your understanding.

## 5 Put into practice

Join in this conversation.

我们星期日有一个晚会。你能来吗?
women xingqiri you yige wanhui. ni neng lai ma
*We are having a party on Saturday. Are you free to come?*

Say: Yes, how nice!

好,那太好了。
hao, na tai hao le

那太好了。
na tai hao le
*That's great!*

Say: At what time should we arrive?

我们几点钟来呢?
women jidianzhong lai ne

谢谢你的邀请。
xiexie ni de yaoqing
*Thank you for inviting us.*

好,那太好了。
hao, na tai hao le

*Yes, how nice!*

请带你的先生一起来。
qing dai ni-de xiansheng yiqilai

*Please bring your husband.*

我们几点钟来呢?
women jidianzhong lai ne

*At what time should we come?*

**Da an**
*Answers*
Cover with flap

# Fuxi yu lianxi
*Review and repeat*

### 1 Animals

1 猫
mao

2 鸟
niao

3 马
ma

4 鱼
yu

5 狗
gou

### 1 Animals

Name the numbered animals in Chinese.

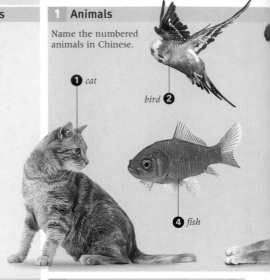

❶ *cat*

*bird* ❷

❹ *fish*

### 2 I like...

1 我想打 球。
wo xiang da bangqiu

2 我想打高尔夫。
wo xiang da gao-er-fu

3 我想画画。
wo xiang huahua

### 2 I like...

Say the following in Chinese:

1 *I like playing baseball.*

2 *I like playing golf.*

3 *I like painting.*

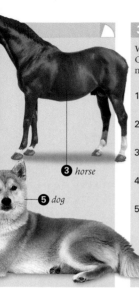

**3** horse

**5** dog

### 3 Leisure

What do these Chinese sentences mean?

1 wo zui bu xihuan kala-ok

2 wo xihuan wan dianzi youxi

3 wo de aihao shi dushu

4 wo bing bu xihuan gouwu

5 wo la xiaotiqin

### 3 Leisure

1 *I hate karaoke.*

2 *I like video games.*

3 *My hobby is reading.*

4 *I don't really like shopping.*

5 *I play the violin.*

### 4 An invitation

You are invited for dinner. Join in the conversation, replying in Chinese following the English prompts.

nin xiang lai canjia xingqiliu de wanyan ma
1 *Sorry, I'm busy on Saturday.*

xingqisi zenmeyang
2 *Yes, how nice!*

qing dai ni de xiansheng yiqilai
3 *At what time should we arrive?*

wanshang badian
4 *Thank you very much.*

### 4 An invitation

1 对不起，我星期六很忙。
duibuqi, wo xingqiliu henmang

2 好，那太好了。
hao, na tai hao le

3 我们几点钟来呢？
women jidianzhong lain ne

4 谢谢你。
xiexie ni

# Reinforce and progress

Regular practice is the key to maintaining and advancing your language skills. In this section, you will find a variety of suggestions for reinforcing and extending your knowledge of Chinese. Many involve returning to exercises in the book and using the dictionary to extend their scope. Go back through the lessons in a different order, mix and match activities to make up your own 15-minute daily programme, or focus on topics that are of particular relevance to your current needs.

**Keep warmed up**

Re-visit the Warm Up boxes to remind yourself of key words and phrases. Make sure you work your way through all of them on a regular basis.

**1  Warm up**

Ask "How much is that?" (pp.18–19)

What are "breakfast", "lunch", and "dinner"? (pp.20–21)

What are "three", "four", "five", and "six"? (pp.10–11)

**2  I'd like...**

Say you'd like the following:

cake **1**

**2** tea

**3** coffee

**4** sugar

**Review and repeat again**

Work through a Review and Repeat lesson as a way of reinforcing words and phrases presented in the course. Return to the main lesson for any topic on which you are no longer confident.

**3  In conversation: taxi**

**Carry on conversing**

Re-read the In Conversation panels. Say both parts of the conversation, paying attention to the pronunciation. Where possible, try incorporating new words from the dictionary.

请带我去故宫, 好吗?
qing daiwo qu gugong, hao ma

*I'd like to go to the Forbidden City, please.*

上车吧。
shangche ba

*Do get in.*

我就在这儿下车, 可以吗?
wo jiu zai zhe er xiache, keyi ma

*Can you drop me here please?*

**4  Useful phrases**

Learn these phrases and then test yourself using the flap.

| | | |
|---|---|---|
| | What time do you open? | 你们什么时间开门? nimen shenme shijian kaimen |
| | What time do you close? | 你们什么时间关门? nimen shenme shijian guanmen |
| | Is wheelchair access possible? | 轮椅可以方便进出吗? lunyi keyi fangbian jinchu ma |

营业

Smart Identity Card Centre
智能身份證中心

**Practise phrases**

Return to the Useful Phrases and Put into Practice exercises. Test yourself using the cover flap. When you are confident, devise your own versions of the phrases, using new words from the dictionary.

**Match, repeat, and extend**
Remind yourself of words related to specific topics by returning to the Match and Repeat and Words to Remember exercises. Test yourself using the cover flap. Discover new words in that area by referring to the dictionary and menu guide.

5 **Match and repeat**

Match the numbered items to the Chinese words in the panel on the left and test yourself using the cover flap.

1 鼠标
  shubiao

2 适配器
  shipeiqi

3 变压器
  bianyaqi

4 笔记本电脑
  bijiben diannao

5 屏幕
  pingmu

6 保修证
  baoxiuzheng

7 内存
  neicun

8 电池
  dianchi

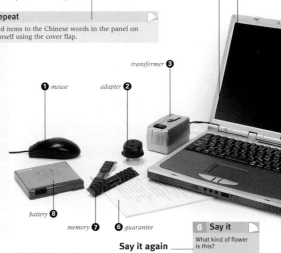

④ laptop
⑤ screen
③ transformer
① mouse
② adapter
⑧ battery
⑦ memory
⑥ guarantee

**Say it again**
The Say It exercises are a useful instant reminder for each lesson. Practise these, using your own vocabulary variations from the dictionary or elsewhere in the lesson.

6 **Say it**
What kind of flower is this?

I like the waterfall.

Is there a pond?

## Using other resources

In addition to working with this book, try the following language extension ideas:

- Visit China if you can and try out your new skills with native speakers. Otherwise, find out if there is a Mandarin-speaking community near you. There may be shops, cafés, restaurants, and clubs. Try to visit some of these and use your Chinese to order food and drink and strike up conversations. Most native speakers will be happy to speak Chinese to you.

- Join a language class or club. There are usually evening and day classes available at a variety of different levels. Or you could start a club yourself if you have friends who are also interested in keeping up their Chinese.

- Practise your new knowledge of the Chinese characters (see pp.152–7). Look at the back of food packages and other products. You will often find a Chinese list of ingredients or components. See if you can spot some familiar characters in the Chinese list and then compare to the English equivalent.

- Look at the titles and advertisements of Chinese magazines and comics. The pictures will help you to decipher the script. Look for familiar words and characters, even if you can't make out the whole text.

- Use the internet to find websites for learning languages, some of which offer free online help.

# Menu guide

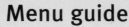

This guide lists the most common terms you may encounter on Chinese menus. Dishes are divided into categories and the Chinese script is displayed clearly to help you identify items on a menu.

## Rice and noodle dishes

| | | |
|---|---|---|
| miantiao | 面条 | *noodles* |
| mifan | 米饭 | *rice* |
| nuomi | 糯米 | *glutinous rice* |
| chaofan | 炒饭 | *fried rice* |
| dan chaofan | 蛋炒饭 | *fried rice with egg* |
| chaomian | 炒面 | *fried noodles* |
| chaomifen | 炒米粉 | *fried rice noodles* |
| zhou | 粥 | *rice porridge* |

## Basic food items

| | | |
|---|---|---|
| chunjuan | 春卷 | *spring rolls* |
| doushabao | 豆沙包 | *steamed dumplings with sweet bean paste filling* |
| huajuan | 花卷 | *steamed rolls* |
| mantou | 馒头 | *steamed bread* |

| mianbao | 面包 | *bread* (white) |
| nailao | 奶酪 | *cheese* |
| rou | 肉 | *meat* (usually pork) |
| xiancai | 咸菜 | *pickles* |

## Cooking methods and combinations

| chao... | 炒... | *stir-fried...* |
| chashao... | 叉烧... | *barbecued...* |
| ...ding | ...丁 | *diced...* |
| donggu... | 冬菇... | *...with dried mushrooms* |
| gali... | 咖喱... | *curried...* |
| gongbao... | 宫保... | *stir-fried... with peanuts and chilli* |
| haoyou... | 蚝油... | *...with oyster sauce* |
| hongshao... | 红烧... | *...braised in brown sauce* |
| hualiu... | 滑溜... | *stir-fried ...with sauce added* |
| hu... | 烩... | *stewed...* |
| huoguo... | 火锅... | *...in hotpot* |
| huotui... | 火腿... | *...with ham* |
| jiachang... | 家常... | *home-style...* |
| kao... | 烤... | *roasted...* |

| ...kuai | ...块 | *...chunks, pieces* |
|---------|------|---------------------|
| lazi... | 辣子... | *...with chilli* |
| majiang... | 麻酱... | *...quick-fried in sesame paste* |
| mala... | 麻辣... | *...with chilli and wild pepper* |
| ...pian | ...片 | *sliced...* |
| fanqiezhi... | 番茄汁... | *...with tomato sauce* |
| qingzheng... | 清蒸... | *steamed...* |
| sanxian... | 三鲜... | *"three-fresh" ... (with three varied ingredients)* |
| ...si | ...丝 | *shredded...* |
| tangcu ...wan (or yuan) | 糖醋...丸 (元) | *sweet and sour... balls* |
| xiangsu... | 香酥... | *crispy deep-fried...* |
| zha... | 炸... | *deep-fried...* |
| zhacai... | 榨菜... | *...with pickled mustard greens* |
| zheng... | 蒸... | *steamed...* |

## Pork

| zhurou | 猪肉 | *pork* |
|--------|------|--------|
| chashao rou | 叉烧肉 | *barbecued pork* |
| fen zhengrou | 粉蒸肉 | *steamed pork with rice* |

| lazi rouding | 辣子肉丁 | *stir-fried diced pork with chilli* |
|---|---|---|
| muxu rou | 木须肉 | *stir-fried sliced pork with eggs, tree-ear (edible fungus), and day lily (type of dried lily)* |
| qingjiao chao roupian | 青椒炒肉片 | *stir-fried sliced pork roupian with pepper* |
| sun chao roupian | 笋炒肉片 | *stir-fried sliced pork with bamboo shoots* |
| tangcu paigu | 糖醋排骨 | *spare ribs cooked in a sweet and sour sauce* |
| zhacai rousi | 榨菜肉丝 | *stir-fried shredded pork with pickled mustard greens* |

## Chicken and duck

| ji | 鸡 | *chicken* |
|---|---|---|
| jiding | 鸡丁 | *diced chicken* |
| jiangbao jiding | 酱爆鸡丁 | *diced chicken quick-fried with bean sauce* |
| baizhanji | 白斩鸡 | *sliced cold chicken* |
| jiaohuaji | 叫化鸡 | *"beggar's chicken" (charcoal-baked marinaded chicken)* |
| ya | 鸭 | *duck* |
| Beijing kaoya | 北京烤鸭 | *Peking roast duck* |
| xianggu yazhang | 香菇鸭掌 | *duck's foot with mushroom* |

## Beef and lamb

| niurou | 牛肉 | beef |
|---|---|---|
| congbao niurou | 葱爆牛肉 | beef quick-fried with Chinese onions |
| gongbao niurou | 宫保牛肉 | stir-fried beef with peanuts and chilli |
| yuxiang niurou | 鱼香牛肉 | stir-fried beef in hot spicy sauce |
| hongshao niurou | 红烧牛肉 | beef braised in brown sauce |
| yangrou | 羊肉 | lamb |
| kao yangrouchuan | 烤羊肉串 | lamb kebabs |
| shuan yangrou | 涮羊肉 | Mongolian hotpot |

## Fish and seafood

| yu | 鱼 | fish |
|---|---|---|
| yupian | 鱼片 | fish slices |
| tangcu yukuai | 糖醋鱼块 | sweet and sour fish |
| hualiu yupian | 滑溜鱼片 | stir-fried fish slices with thick sauce added |
| xia | 虾 | prawns |
| furong xiaren | 芙蓉虾仁 | stir-fried prawns with egg white |
| youyu | 鱿鱼 | squid |
| liyu | 鲤鱼 | carp |

| qingzheng liyu | 清蒸鲤鱼 | *steamed carp* |
| hongshao liyu | 红烧鲤鱼 | *carp braised in brown sauce* |
| sansi yuchi | 三丝鱼翅 | *shark's fin with shredded sea cucumber, abalone, and bamboo shoots* |
| ganshao huangshan | 干烧黄鳝 | *eel braised with chilli and bean sauce* |

## Vegetables

| baicai | 白菜 | *cabbage* |
| bocai | 菠菜 | *spinach* |
| caihua | 菜花 | *cauliflower* |
| douya | 豆芽 | *bean sprouts* |
| chao douya | 炒豆芽 | *stir-fried bean sprouts* |
| mogu | 蘑菇 | *mushroom* |
| yumi | 玉米 | *corn* |
| qiezi | 茄子 | *aubergine* |
| tudou | 土豆 | *potato* |
| tudoutiao | 土豆条 | *chips* |
| xihongshi | 西红柿 | *tomato* |
| xihongshi chao jidan | 西红柿炒鸡蛋 | *stir-fried tomato with egg* |
| chao shicai | 炒时菜 | *stir-fried seasonal vegetables* |

| | | |
|---|---|---|
| dongsun biandou | 冬笋扁豆 | *stir-fried French beans with bamboo shoots* |
| su shijin | 素什锦 | *stir-fried assorted vegetables* |
| xianmo wandou | 鲜蘑豌豆 | *stir-fried peas with mushrooms* |

## *Specialities*

| | | |
|---|---|---|
| baozi | 包子 | *steamed dumplings with minced pork or various fillings* |
| chashaobao | 叉烧包 | *steamed dumplings with barbecued pork filling* |
| xiaolongbao | 小笼包 | *steamed dumplings with various fillings* |
| doufu | 豆腐 | *bean curd* |
| doufu gan | 豆腐干 | *dried bean curd* |
| doufu pi | 豆腐皮 | *dried soy bean cream* |
| guoba doufu | 锅巴豆腐 | *bean curd fried in batter* |
| xiaren doufu | 虾仁豆腐 | *bean curd with prawns* |
| sanxian doufu | 三鲜豆腐 | "three-fresh" bean curd (with three varied ingredients) |
| mapo doufu | 麻婆豆腐 | "pock-marked woman bean curd" (bean curd with minced beef in hot spicy sauce) |
| fuzhu | 腐竹 | "bean curd bamboo" (dried soy bean cream, in the shape of bamboo) |

| | | |
|---|---|---|
| shuijiao | 水饺 | *Chinese ravioli* |
| zhengjiao | 蒸饺 | *steamed Chinese ravioli* |
| guotie | 锅贴 | *fried Chinese ravioli* |
| huntun (or yuntun or chaoshou) | 混沌 | *small Chinese ravioli in soup* |
| songhuadan | 松花蛋 | *preserved eggs* |
| xianbing | 馅饼 | *savoury fritter* |
| youtiao | 油条 | *unsweetened doughnut sticks* |

## Soups

| | | |
|---|---|---|
| zicai tang | 紫菜汤 | *seaweed and dried prawn soup* |
| sanxian tang | 三鲜汤 | *"three-fresh" soup (normally prawn, meats, and a seasonal vegetable)* |
| shicai roupian tang | 时菜肉片汤 | *soup with sliced pork and seasonal vegetables* |
| shijin donggua tang | 什锦冬瓜汤 | *winter marrow soup* |
| bocai fensi tang | 菠菜粉丝汤 | *soup with spinach and vermicelli* |
| xihongshi jidan tang | 西红柿鸡蛋汤 | *soup with eggs and tomato* |
| zhacai rousi tang | 榨菜肉丝汤 | *soup with shredded pork and pickled mustard greens* |

## Fruit

| | | |
|---|---|---|
| boluo | 菠萝 | *pineapple* |
| guanggan | 广柑 | *Guangdong sweet orange* |
| hamigua | 哈密瓜 | *honeydew melon* |
| juzi (or miju) | 橘子<br>(蜜橘) | *tangerine* |
| li | 梨 | *pear* |
| lizhi | 荔枝 | *lychee* |
| pingguo | 苹果 | *apple* |
| putao | 葡萄 | *grape* |
| xiangjiao | 香蕉 | *banana* |
| xigua | 西瓜 | *watermelon* |

## Desserts

| | | |
|---|---|---|
| basi xiangjiao | 拔丝香蕉 | *banana fritters* |
| bingqilin | 冰淇淋 | *ice cream* |
| shuiguo sela | 水果色拉 | *fruit salad* |
| shijin shuiguo geng | 什锦水果羹 | *fruit salad soup* |
| babao fan | 八宝饭 | *"eight-treasure" rice dessert (with eight types of fruit and nuts)* |
| bingtang yin'er | 冰糖银耳 | *silver tree-ear (edible fungus) in syrup* |

# *Drinks*

| shui | 水 | *water* |
|------|-----|---------|
| guozhi | 果汁 | *fruit juice* |
| cha | 茶 | *tea* |
| kafei | 咖啡 | *coffee* |
| niunai | 牛奶 | *milk* |
| doujiang | 豆浆 | *soya milk* |
| qishui | 汽水 | *aerated water* |
| baijiu | 白酒 | *baijiu* (a clear spirit) |
| pijiu | 啤酒 | *beer* |
| putaojiu | 葡萄酒 | *wine* |

# Dictionary
## *English* to Chinese

This dictionary contains the vocabulary from *15-Minute Chinese*, together with many other high-frequency words. You can also find additional terms for food and drink in the Menu Guide (pp.128–137).

In Chinese, the plural of nouns is normally the same as the singular. Chinese descriptive words, or adjectives, may have different endings depending on how they are used and are also often preceded by hen (*"very"*). Verbs have no tenses and don't generally change according to who or what is the subject; but there are some characters that can be added to indicate a particular time or mood – see p.112.

## A

*a* (one) yige
*accident* shigu
*accountant* kuaijishi
*ache* teng
*actor* yanyuan
*adaptor* (plug) zhuanjie chatou
*address* dizhi
*admission: admission charge* menpiao fei
  *admission ticket* menpiao
*after* yihou
*afternoon* xiawu
*again* zai
*agenda* huiyi richeng
*air conditioning* kongtiao
*air mail* hangkong youjian
*airport* jichang, feijichang
*alarm clock* naozhong
*alcohol* jiujing
*all* suoyou
  *all the streets* suoyou de jiedao
  *that's all, thanks* haole, xiexie
*allergic* guomin
*almost* chabuduo
*alone* dandu
*already* yijing
*also* ye
*always* zongshi
*am: I am* wo shi
*America* meiguo

*American* (person) meiguo ren
*and* he
*animal* dongwu
*another* (different) ling yige
  (further) you yige
*anniversary* zhounian
*answering machine* liuyanji
*antibiotics* kangshengsu
*antique shop* gudongdian
*antiseptic* fangfuji
*anything: anything else?* haiyao qita shipin ma?
*apartment* gongyu, danyuan
*apple* pingguo
*appointment book* riji
*April* siyue
*architecture* (study) jianzhuxue
*are: you are* ni shi
  *we are* women shi
  *they are* tamen shi
*arm* shoubi, gebo
*arrival* daoda
*arrive* daoda
*art* yishu
*ashtray* yanhuigang
*asleep: he's asleep* ta shuizhao le
*ask* wen
*asthma* xiaochuanbing

*at* zai
  *at the café* zai kafei guan
*attic* gelou
*attractive* mirende
*August* bayue
*aunt* (maternal) yima
  (paternal) guma
*Australia* aodaliya
*Australian* (adj) aodaliya
*autumn* qiu
*awful* zaotoule

## B

*baby* ying'er
*baby wipes* ying'er caxijin
*back* (body) bei
*backpack* beibao
*back street* houjie
*bad* huai
*bag* (for purchases, etc.) suliaodai
*baggage* xingle
*baker* mianbaolei, mianbaodian
*balcony* yangtai
*ball* qiu
*bamboo* zhuzi
*bamboo shoots* zhusun
*banana* xiangjiao
*band* (music) yuedui
*bandage* bengdai
*bank* yinhang
*banknote* zhibi
*bar* jiuba

*barber* lifadian
*baseball* bangqiu
*basketball* lanqiu
*bath* yugang, xizao
*bathroom* weishengjian, xizaojian
*battery* dianchi
*beach* haitan
*beans* dou
*beard* luosaihuzi
*beautiful* meili, haokan
*beauty products* huazhuangpin
*because* yinwei
*bed* chuang
*bed runner* chuangqi
*bedroom* woshi
*bedside table* chuangtougui
*bedspread* chuangdan
*beef* niurou
*beer* pijiu
*before*(zai) ... yiqian
*begin* kaishi
*behind* (zai) ... houmian
*bell* zhong
  (for door, school) ling
*below* (zai) ... xiamian
*belt* (clothing) yaodai
*best: the best* zuihao
*better* geng hao
*between* (zai) ... zhijian
*bicycle* zixingche
*big* da
*bikini* bijini
*bill* zhangdan
*bird* niao
*birthday* shengri
  *happy birthday!* shengri kuaile!
*biscuit* binggan
*bite* yao
*bitter* (taste) ku
*black* hei
*blanket* maotan, tanzi
*blind* xia
*blinds* baiye chuang
*blocked* (road, drain) duzhule
*blond* (adj) jinhuangse
*blood test* yanxue
*blouse* nvchenshan
*blue* lan

*boarding pass* dengjipai
*boat* chuan
*body* shenti
*boiled* zhu
*boiled rice* mifan
*bonnet* (of car) fadongjigai
*book* (noun) shu
*book* (verb) ding
*bookshop* shudian, tushulei
*boot* xuezi
  (car) houcang
*border* (of country) bianjie
*boring* mei jing
*boss* laoban
*both* liangge dou
*bottle* pingzi
*bottle opener* ping gai kai dao
*bowl* wan
*box* hezi
*boxer* quanjishou
*boy* nanhai
*boyfriend* nan pengyou
*bra* xiongzhao
*bracelet* shouzhuo
*branch* (of company) fenzhi jigou
*brandy* bailandi
*bread* mianbao
*breakfast* zaocan
*bridge* (over river, etc.) daqiao
*briefcase* gongwenbao
*bring* dai
*Britain* yingguo
*British* (adj) yingguo
*broken* (out of order) huai le
  (leg) duanle
*brooch* xiongzhen
*brother* (older) gege
  (younger) didi
*brown* zongse
*bruise* shanghen
*brush* shuazi
*Buddha* Fo
*budget* yusuan
*building* loufang
*bulb* (light) deng pao
*bumper* baoxiangang
*bungalow* pingfang
*burglar* pashou, qiezei

*Burma* miandian
*burn* (noun) shaoshang
*bus* gonggong qiche
*business* shengyi
*business card* mingpian
*businessperson* shangren
*bus station* gonggong qiche zong zhan
*bus stop* chezhan
*busy* (street) renao
  (person) hen mang
  (phone line) zhanxian
*but* danshi
*butcher* roulei, roudian
*butter* huangyou
*button* niukou
*buy* mai
*by* zou
  *by train/car* zuo huoche/zuo qiche

# C

*cabinet* (kitchen) guichu
*cable TV* youxian dianshi
*café* kafei ting, chaguan
*cake* dangao
*cake shop* gaodianlei
*calculator* jisuanqi
*call: what is this called?* zhe jiao shenme?
*calligraphy* shufa
*camera* zhaoxiangji
*can* (tin) guantou
*can: can I ...?* wo keyi ... ma?
  *can you ...?* ni neng bu neng ...?
  *he can't ...* ta bu neng ...
*can opener* guantou qizi
*Canada* jianada
*candle* lazhu
*canopy* yulian
*Cantonese* (adj) Guangdong
  (language) Guangdonghua
*cap* maozi

car qiche, che
  *car park*
  tingchechang
card (business)
  mingpian
*cards* (playing) pu-ke
*careful: be careful!*
  xiaoxin!
*carpenter* mujiang
*carpet* ditan
*car seat* (for a baby)
  ying'er qiche anquan
  zuoyi
cash (money) xianjin
*cash point* zidong
  tikuanji
*cassette* cidai
*cat* mao
*CD-drive* guangqu
ceiling tianhuaban
centre (of town)
  zhongxin
chair yizi
  *swivel chair* zuoyi
change (verb: money)
  huanqian, duihuan
  (noun: money)
  lingqian
  (verb: clothes,
  trains) huan
charger chongdianqi
check-in banli dengji
  shouxu
cheque zhipiao
chequebook zhipiaoben
cheque card zhipiaoka
cheese nailao
chef chushi
chemist (pharmacy)
  yaofang
chess xiang-qi
chest (body) xiong
chewing gum
  kouxiangtang
chicken ji
  (meat) jirou
child, children haizi
children's ward xiaoer
  bingfang
chilli powder lajiaofen
China zhongguo
*China tea* zhongguo
  cha

*Chinese* (adj) zhongguo
  (person) zhongguo
  ren
  (language) Hanyu
  *the Chinese* zhongguo
  renmin
*Chinese New Year*
  zhongguo chunjie
*Chinese-style* zhongshi
*chips* zha tudoutiao
*chocolate* qiaokeli
*chopsticks* kuaizi
*church* jiaotang
*cigar* xuejia
*cigarette* xiang yan
*cinema* dianyingyuan
*city* chengshi
*clean* (adj) ganjing
*cleaner* (person)
  qingjiegong
*clever* congming
*clock* zhong
*close* (verb) guan
*close: to be close* (near)
  jin
*closed* guanle, xiuxi
*clothes* yifu
*clothes peg* yifu jiazi
*coach* (train) chexiang
  *sleeper coach* yingwo
  chexiang
  *ordinary coach*
  putong chexiang
*coast* haibin
*coat* (overcoat) dayi
  (jacket) waiyi
*coat hanger* yijia
*cockroach* zhanglang
*coconut* yezi
*coconut milk* yezi zhi
*coffee* kafei
*coins* yingbi
*cold* (illness) ganmao
  (temperature) leng
*collect/reverse charge call*
  duifang fukuan
*colour* yanse
*comb* shuzi
*come* lai
  *come in!* qing jin
  *please come!* lai ba!
*Communist Party*
  gongchandang
*Communist Party*
  *member*
  gongchandangyuan
*company* (firm) gongsi

*complicated* fuza
*computer* diannao,
  jisuanji
*computer repair shop*
  diannao xiulidian
*concert* yinyuehui
*condom* biyuntao
*conference* yantaohui
*consulate* lingshiguan
*contact lenses* yinxing
  yanjing
*contract* (noun)
  hetong
*cool* (day, weather)
  liangkuai
*cook* (chef) chushi
*corner* (street) jiejiao
*corridor* zoulang
*cost* jia qian
  *what does it cost?* zhe
  yao duoshao qian?
*cot* diao
  chuang/ying'er
  chuang
*cotton* mianhua
*cotton wool* yaomian
*cough* kesou
*country* (nation)
  guojia
*cow* niu
*crab* pangxie
*cramp* jingluan
*cream* (to eat) naiyou
*credit card* xinyongka
*crime* fanzui
*crisps* zha tudoupian
*crocodile* eyu
*crossing* (street)
  banmaxian
*crowd* renqun
*crowded* yongji
*Cultural Revolution*
  wenhua dageming
*cup* beizi
  *a cup of coffee* yi bei
  kafei
*curry* gali
*curtains* chuanglian
*customs* haiguan
*cut* qie
*cyclist* qi zixingche de
  ren

# D

*dairy* (products)
  ruzhipin

*dangerous* weixian

*dark* hei an

*daughter* nv-er

*day* tian

*dead* sile

*deaf* er long

*December* shieryue

*deep* shen

*delayed* wandian

*delicatessen* shushilei

*delicious* haochi

*delivery* jiaofu

*dentist* yayi, yake yisheng

*deodorant* chuchouji

*department* (of company) bu

*department store* baihuo shangdian, baihuodalou

*departure(s)* chufa

*designer* shejishi

*desk* bangongzhuo

*desserts* taindian

*develop* (film) chongxi

*diabetes* tangniaobing

*diarrhoea* laduzi

*diary* rizhi

*dictionary* zidian

*die* si

*different* butong

*difficult* kunnan

*dining room* canting

*dinner* wancan

*dinner party* wanyan

*dirty* zang

*disabled* canfei

*disco* disike

*dish washer* xiwanji

*disposable nappies* yicixing niaojin

*divorced* lihunle

*do* zuo

*doctor* yisheng

*document* wenjian

*dog* gou

*dollar* meiyuan

*don't!* buyao!

*door* men (vehicle) chemen

*double room* shuangren fang

*drawer* chouti

*down: down there* xiamian

*dress* (woman's) lianyiqun

*dressing gown* chenyi

*drink* (verb) he

*drinking water* yinyongshui

*drinks* (catagory) yinliao

*driving licence* jiazhao

*drops* (medicinal) yaoshui

*drunk* hezuile

*dry* gan

*dry cleaner's* ganxidian

*dynasty* chao dai the Ming/Ch'ing Dynasty mingchao/ qingchao

# E

*each* mei yige

*ear* erduo

*earphones* erji

*early* zao

*earring* erhuan

*east* dong

*easy* rongyi

*eat* chi

*egg* jidan

*egg noodles* jidan mian

*eight* ba, ba-ge

*either … or …* bu shi … jiushi …

*elastic* you tanxing de

*elbow* zhou

*electrician* diangong

*electricity* dian, gongdian

*electronics store* dianqi shangdian

*else: something else* biede dongxi *anything else?* haiyao qita shipin ma? *somewhere else* biede difang

*email* dianzi youjian

*email address* dianzi youzhi

*embarrassing* ganga

*embassy* dashiguan

*emergency* jinji qingkuang

*emergency ward* jizhenshi

*emperor* huangdi

*empty* kong

*end* (noun) moduan

*engaged* (to be married) dinghunle

*engine* fadongji

*engineer* gongchengshi

*engineering* (study) gong-ke

*England* yingguo

*English* (person) yingguo ren (language) yingyu

*enough* goule

*entrance* rukou, ruchang

*envelope* xinfeng

*epilepsy* dianxianzheng

*eraser* xiangpi

*estimate* gusuan

*evening* wanshang

*every* meiyige *every day* meitian *every week* meixingqi

*everyone* meiyige ren

*everything* meijian shiqing

*everywhere* meige difang

*excellent* haojile

*exchange* (goods) genghuan

*exchange rate* huilv

*excuse me* (to get attention) qingwen, lao jia (pardon?) qing zai shuo yibian, hao ma?

*exhibition* zhanshihui

*exit* chukou

*expensive* gui

*eye* yan, yanjing

*eyebrow* mei

*eye-witness* mujizhe

# F

*face* lian

*factory* gongchang

*family* jiating

*fan* (mechanical) fengshan (hand-held) shanzi

*far* (away) yuan

*fare* chepiao

*farmer* nongmin

*fashion* shiyang

*fast* kuai

*fat* (person) pang

*father* fuqin
  *my father* baba

*fax* chuanzhen

*fax machine*
  chuanzhenji

*February* eryue

*feel* ganjue
  *I feel hot* wo juede re

*ferry* duchuan

*fever* fashao

*few: a few* yixie

*fiance(e)* wei hun fu/qi

*field* tiandi
  (rice, paddy)
  daotian

*figures* (e.g. sales)
  zongji

*film* (camera) jiaojuan
  (movie) dianying

*find* zhao

*finger* shou zhitou

*fire* huo
  *there's a fire!*
  zhaohuo la!

*fire extinguisher*
  miehuoqi

*first* diyi

*fish* yu

*fisherman* yumin

*fishmonger* yulei

*fishing* diaoyu

*fishing boat* yuchuan

*fizzy* youqide

*five* wu, wu-ge

*flag* qizi

*flash* (for camera)
  shanguangdeng

*flat* (adj) pingtan

*flat tyre* chetai meiqi le

*flavour* weidao

*flea* tiaozao

*flight* hangban

*floor* (of room) diban
  (storey) lou

*florist* huahuidian

*flower* hua, hua'er

*fly* (insect) cangying

*fly* (verb) fei

*flyover* lijiaoqiao

*folk music* minjian
  yinyue

*food* shiwu

*food poisoning* shiwu
  zhongdu

*foot* jiao
  *foot treatment* (spa)
  zuliao

*football* zuqiu

*for: for her* wei ta
  *that's for me* zhe shi
  gei wode
  *a bus for …* qu … de
  gonggong qiche

*forbidden* jinzhi

*Forbidden City* gugong

*foreigner* waiguo ren

*forest* senlin

*fork* chazi

*four* si, si-ge

*fountain* penquan

*fracture* guzhe

*free* (of charge)
  mianfei
  *to be free* (available)
  you kong

*freezer* binggui

*Friday* xingqiwu

*fridge* bingxiang

*fried* chao

*fried noodles* chaomian

*fried rice* chaofan

*friend* pengyou

*friendly* qinre ren

*friendship store* youyi
  shangdian

*from: from Beijing to
  Shanghai*
  cong beijing dao
  shanghai

*front* qianmian

*frozen foods*
  lengdongshipin

*fruit* shuiguo

*fruit juice* guozhi

*fry* (deep fry) zha
  (stir fry) chao

*full* man
  *I'm full* wo baole

*funny* (strange) qiguai
  (amusing) you yisi

*furniture* jiaju

# G

*garden* huayuan

*garlic* dasuan

*gate* (airport, etc.)
  dengjikou

*get* (obtain) de dao

*get* (fetch) qu
  (train, bus, etc)
  zuoche

*get: have you got …?* ni
  you … ma?

*get in* (to car)
  shangche
  (arrive) daoda

*get up* (in morning)
  qichuang

*gift* liwu

*ginger* shengjiang

*girl* nvhai

*girlfriend* nvpengyou

*give* gei

*glad* gaoxing

*glass* (for drinking)
  juibei, beizi
  (material) boli

*glasses* (spectacles)
  yanjing
  *wearing glasses*
  daiyanjing

*glue* jiaoshui

*go* qu

*gold* huangjin

*golf/golfer* gao-er-fu

*golf course* gao-er-fu
  qiuchang

*good* hao

*good morning*
  zaoshang hao

*good evening*
  wanshang hao

*good night* wan an

*goodbye* zaijian

*government* zhengfu

*granddaughter*
  (son's daughter)
  sunnv
  (daughter's
  daughter) waisunnv

*grandfather*
  (paternal) yeye
  (maternal) waigong

*grandmother*
  (paternal) nainai
  (maternal) waipo

*grandson* (son's son)
  sunzi
  (daughter's son) wai
  sunzi

*grapes* putao

*grass* cao

*great: that's great!* hao
  ji le, na tai hao le

*Great Britain*
dabuliedian

*Great Wall*
changcheng

*green* lv

*greengrocer* shucailei

*green Chinese onion*
dacong

*green tea* lvcha

*grey* huise

*grilled* shao

*ground floor* yi lou

*guarantee* baoxiuzheng

*guest* keren

*guide* daoyou

*guidebook* daoyou ce

*guided tour* tuanti
canguan

*gun* (pistol)
shouqiang
(rifle) qiang

*gutter* (of house)
tiangou

# H

*hair* toufa

*hair dryer*
dianchuifeng

*haircut* lifa

*hairdresser* meifadian

*half* ban
*half past one* yidian
ban

*ham* huotui

*hamburger* hanbaobao

*hammer* chuizi

*hand* shou

*hand towel* maojin

*handbag* shoutibao

*handkerchief* shoujuan

*handle* (noun) bashou

*handsome* yingjun

*handyman* xiuligong

*happen* fasheng

*happy* kuaile

*harbour* gangkou

*hard* (material) ying
(difficult) nan

*hard drive* yingpan

*hat* maozi

*hate: I hate …* wo zui
bu xihuan …

*have* you
*do you have …?* ni
you … ma?
*I don't have …* wo
mei you …

*hay fever* huafenre

*he* ta

*head* tou

*head office* zongbu

*headache* tou teng

*headlights* qiandeng

*hear* tingjian

*hearing aid*
zhutingqi

*heart* xinzang

*heart condition*
xinzangbing

*heat(ing)* gongnuan

*heavy* zhong

*heel* (shoe) xiegen
(foot) jiaogen

*hello* nihao
(on the phone) wei

*help* (verb) bangzhu

*help!* jiuming!

*hepatitis* ganyan

*her* (possessive) ta-de
(object) ta

*herbs* (cooking)
zuoliao
(medicine) caoyao

*here* zheli, zhe er
*here you are* zhebian
qing

*hers* tade

*hi!* ni hao!

*high* gao

*hill* xiaoshan

*him* ta

*his* ta-de

*HIV positive* aizibing
yangxing

*hobby* aihao

*holiday* jiaqi
*on holiday* dujia
(public) jieri

*home* jia

*homosexual*
tongxinglian

*Hong Kong* xianggang

*horrible* kepa

*horse* ma

*hospital* yiyuan

*host* dongdaozhu

*hot* re
(to taste) la

*hot spa* wenquan dujia

*hotel* (superior, for
foreigners) jiudian
(small) lvguan

*hour* xiaoshi

*house* fangzi

*household products*
jiatingyongpin

*how?* zenme?

*how long?: how long
does it take?*
xuyao duojiu?

*how much?* duo shao?
(money) duo shao
qian?

*hundred* bai

*hungry: I'm hungry* wo
ele

*hurry: I'm in a hurry*
wo mei shijian

*hurt* teng

*husband* zhangfu

# I

*I* wo

*ice* bing

*ice cream* bingqilin

*if* ruguo

*ill* sheng bingle

*immediately* mashang

*impossible* bu keneng

*in* zai
*in English* yong
yingyu

*India* yindu

*indigestion*
xiaohuabuliang

*inexpensive* pianyi

*inhaler* (for asthma,
etc) xiruqi

*infection* ganran

*information* xinxi,
xiaoxi

*information desk* wen
xun chu

*insect repellent*
quchongji

*insurance* baoxian

*interesting* you yisi

*internet* yintewang

*internet café* wangba

*interpret* zuo fanyi

*invitation* yaoqing

*invoice* fapiao

*Ireland* ai'erlan

*iron* (for clothes)
yundou

*is* shi
   *he/she/it is* ta shi
*island* dao
*it* ta
   *it's expensive* gui

# J

*jack* (for car) qianjinding
*jacket* jiakeshan, waitao
*jade* yu
*January* yiyue
*Japan* riben
*jasmine tea* huacha
*jeans* niuzaiku
*jeweller* zhubaodian
*jewellery* shoushi
*job* gongzuo
*jug* guan
*July* qiyue
*June* liuyue
*junk* (boat) fanchuan
*just* (only) jinjin
   *just one* jiu yige

# K

*karaoke* kala-ok
   *karaoke bar* kala-ok ting
*key* yaoshi
*keyboard* jianpan
*kick* (verb) ti
*kilo* gongjin
*kilometre* gongli
*kitchen* chufang
*knee* xi
*knife* dao
*know: I don't know* wo bu zhidao
*Korea: North Korea* bei chaoxian
   *South Korea* nan chaoxian, hanguo

# L

*lady* nvshi
*lake* hu
*lamp* deng, diandeng
*lane* xiaoxiang
*Laos* laowo
*laptop* (computer) bijiben diannao

*large* da
*last* (previous) shang yige
   *last month* shanggeyue
   (final) zuihou
*last name* xing
*last year* qunian
*late* (at night) wan
   (behind schedule), wandian le, chi
*later* yihou
*law* (study) falv
*lawyer* lvshi
*lecture* (university) jiangzuo
*lecture theatre* jiaoshi
*lecturer* (university) daxuejiangshi
*left* (not right) zuo
   *on the left* zai zuobian
*leg* tui
*leisure time* xiuxian yule
*lemon* ningmeng
*lemonade* ningmeng qishui
*letter* (in post) xinjian
*letter box* xinxiang
*lettuce* woju, shengcai
*library* tushuguan
*lie down* tang
*life* shenghuo
*lift* (elevator) dianti
   *could you give me a lift?* ni neng bu neng rang wo dage che?
*light* (noun) deng
   *have you got a light?* jie ge huo, xing ma?
   (not heavy) qing
*light bulb* dengpao
*lighter* dahuoji
*like: I'd like* qing geiwo/wo xiang ...
   *I like* wo xihuan
   *the one like that* xiang neige yiyang
*line* (phone) xian
   *outside line* waixian
   (transport route) lu
*lipstick* kouhong
*literature* (study) wen-ke
*litre* sheng

*little* xiao
   *just a little* jiu yidiandian
*liver* gan
*living roon* keting
*lobster* longxia
*long* chang
*lose: I've lost my ...* wo ... diule
*lost property* shiwu zhaoling chu
*lot: a lot* xuduo
   *a lot of money* xu duo qian
*loud* dasheng de
*love: I love you* wo ai ni
   *I'd love to come* wo yiding lai
*lovely* (person) ke ai
   (thing) hen hao
*low* di
*luck* yunqi
   *good luck!* zhu ni hao yun!
*luggage* xingli
*luggage storage* xingli jicunchu
*lunch* wucan

# M

*make* zuo
*make-up* huazhuangpin
*main courses* zhushi
*man* nanren, nanshi
*manager* jingli
*Mandarin* putonghua
*map* ditu
*March* sanyue
*market* shichang
*married: I'm married* wo jiehunle
*martial arts* wushu
*massage* anmo
*matches* huochai
*material* (cloth) bu
*matter: what's the matter?* (asking about illness) nali bu shufu?
*May* wuyue
*me* wo
   *it's for me* zhe shi gei wode
*meat* rou
*mechanic* jixieshi

*medicine* (medication) yao

*medicine* (study) yi-ke

*meet* (someone) jian

*meeting* huiyi

*melon* gua

*memory* (computer) neicun

*men's toilets* nan cesuo

*menu* caidan
  *set menu* taocan

*metre* mi

*middle: in the middle* zai zhongjian

*middle-aged* zhongnian

*midnight: at midnight* banye

*mile* yingli

*milk* niunai

*million* baiwan

*mine: it's mine* shi wode

*mineral water* kuangquanshui

*minute* fen

*mirror* jingzi

*Miss* xiaojie

*mistake* cuowu

*mobile phone* shouji

*modem* shujuji, tiaozhijietiaoqi

*Monday* xingqiyi

*money* qian

*Mongolia* menggu
  *Inner Mongolia* neimeng
  *Outer Mongolia* waimeng

*monkey* hou

*month* yue

*moon* yueliang

*more* geng duo
  *more than* bi ... duo

*morning* shangwu, zaoshang

*mosquito* wenzi

*mosquito net* (on door) shamen
  (on window) shachuang

*mother* muqin
  *my mother* mama

*motorbike* motuoche

*mountain* shan

*mountain climbing* dengshan

*mouse* (computer) shubiao
  (animal) xiaoshu

*moustache* xiaohuzi

*mouth* zui, zuiba

*Mr ... ...* xiansheng

*Mrs ... ...* furen

*Ms ... ...* nvshi

*much* duo
  *much better* hao de duo

*museum* bowuguan

*mushrooms* mogu

*music* yinyue

*must: I must* wo bixu

*my ... ...* wo-de ...
  *my name ...* wo-de mingzi ...

# N

*name* mingzi

*nappies* niaojin

*narrow* zhai

*near* jin
  *is it near here?* li zheli jin ma?

*nearby* fujin

*necessary* biyao

*neck* bozi

*necklace* xianglian

*need: I need a ...* wo xuyao ..., wo xiang ...

*needle* zhen

*Nepal* niboer

*nephew* zhizi

*never* conglai bu

*new* xin

*news* xinwen

*newspaper* baozhi

*New Year* xinnian
  *Happy New Year!* xinnianhao

*New Zealand* xin xilan

*next* xia yige
  *next month* xiageyue
  *next to ...* zai ... pangbian

*nice* (person, weather) hen hao
  (meal) haochi
  (town) hen hao
  *how nice!* na tai hao le!

*niece* zhinv

*night* ye
  (stay in hotel) tian

*nine* jiu, jiu-ge

*no* bu
  *no entry* jinzhi jinru
  *no parking* jinzhi tingche

*noisy* chaonao

*noodles* maintiao

*noon: at noon* zhongwu

*normal* zhengchang

*north* bei

*nose* bizi

*not* bu
  *not for me* wo bu yao

*notepad* shuxiezhi

*nothing* mei you shenme

*November* shiyiyue

*now* xianzai

*number* (quantity) shuzi
  (numeral) haoma
  *telephone number* dianhua haoma

*nurse* hushi

*nuts* jianguo

# O

*occupied* (toilets) youren

*o'clock ...*dian

*October* shiyue

*of ... ...* de
  *the name of the hotel* lvguande mingzi

*office* bangongshi

*office worker* bagong renyuan

*off-licence* jiulei

*often* jingchang

*oil* (motor) jiyou
  (vegetable) caiyou

*ointment* yaogao

*OK* hao

*old* (person) lao
  (things) jiu

*on* zai ... shangmian
  *on the roof* zai fangding
  *on the beach* zai haitan

*one* yi, yi-ge
  *that one* nei yi-ge

*onion* yangcong

*only* zhi you

*open* (verb) kai
  (adj) kaile

*operating theatre* shoushushi

*operator* (phone) zongji

*opera* geju
  *Chinese opera* jingju

*opposite* duimian
  *opposite the ...* zai ... duimian

*optician* yanjingdian

*or* huozhe

*orange* (fruit) ganju
  (colour) juhuangse

*orange juice* juzhi

*order* (for goods, etc) dinggou, dingdan

*other: the other* ling yige

*other (ones)* qita

*our(s)* women-de

*out: she's out* ta bu zai

*outside* waimian

*over: over there* zai nali

*own: on my own* ziji

*oyster* hao

# P

*pack* (of cigarettes, etc) bao

*package* baoguo

*paddy field* daotian

*page* ye

*pagoda* baota

*pain* teng

*painting* (hobby) huahua

*pair* yishuang

*panda* xiongmao

*paper* zhi

*parasol* yangsan

*pardon?* ni shuo shenme?

*parcel* youbao

*parents* fumu

*park* (noun) gongyuan
  (verb) tingche

*parking space* cheku

*party* (celebration) wanhui
  (group) tuanti

*pass* (mountain) guankou

*passenger* chengke

*passport* huzhao

*passport control* bianfang jiancha

*password* mima

*patient* (hospital, doctor, etc) bingren

*path* xiaolu

*pavement* renxingdao

*pavilion* tingzi

*pay* fuqian
  *can I pay, please?* wo keyi fuqian ma?

*payment* fukuan

*pen* bi

*pencil* qianbi

*penicillin* qingmeisu

*penknife* xiaodao

*people* ren

*pepper* (spice) hujiao
  (red/green) shizijiao

*per: ... per cent* baifen zhi ...

*perfume* xiangshui

*perhaps* keneng

*perm* diantang

*person* ren

*petrol* qiyou, shiyou

*petrol station* jiayouzhan

*pharmacy* yaofang

*phonecard* dianhua ka

*photocopy* fuyin

*photocopier* fuyinji

*photograph* (noun) zhaopian
  (verb) zhaoxiang

*photographer* sheyingshi

*phrase book* duihua shouce

*physics* (study) wulixue

*pickpocket* pashou

*picture* tupian

*piece* pian
  *a piece of ...* yipian ...

*pig* zhu

*pillow* zhentou

*pin* biezhen

*pineapple* boluo

*pink* fenhong

*pipe* (smoking) yandou
  (water) guanzi

*place* difang

*plane* feiji

*plant* zhiwu

*plaster* (sticking) chuangketie

*plastic bag* suliaodai

*plate* candie, panzi

*platform* zhantai

*play* (in theatre) huaju

*play* (verb) (sports, etc) da
  (instrument) la

*please: yes, please* keyi, qing
  *please?* hao ma?

*pleased* gaoxing

*plug* (electric) chatou

*plumber* guandaogong

*pocket* yidai

*poisonous* youdude

*police* jingcha

*police officer* jingguan

*police report* jingfang baogao

*police station* jingchaju

*polite* you limao

*politics* zhengzhi

*pond* chitang

*pool* shuichi

*poor* (not rich) qiong

*pop music* liuxing yinyue

*pork* zhurou

*porter* (hotel) menfang
  (station, etc) banyun gongren

*possible* keneng

*post* youjian

*post office* youju

*postbox* youxiang

*postcard* mingxinpian

*postman* youdiyuan

*poster* zhaotie

*potato* tudou

*pound* (money) yingbang

*prawn* daixia

*pregnant* huaiyun

*present* (gift) liwu

*pretty* piaoliang

*price* jiage

*printer* (machine) dayinji

*problem* wenti

*professor* jiaoshou

*profits* lirun

*pronounce* fayin

*pull* la
*purse* qianbao
*push* tui
*pyjamas* shuiyi

# Q

*quarter* yike
  *quarter past one*
  yidian yike
  *quarter to two* yidian
  sanke
*question* wenti
*queue* (noun) dui
*quick* kuai
*quiet* (place, hotel,
  etc) anjing
*quite: quite a lot* xiang
  dang duo

# R

*rabbit* tu
*radiator* sanreqi
*radio* shouyinji
*railway* tielu
*rain* yu
  *it's raining* xiayu le
*rash* (on body) zhenzi
*rat* laoshu
*raw* shengchi
*razor* tidao
*razor blades* tihu
  daopian
*read* du
*reading* (pastime)
  dushu
*ready* zhunbei hao
*ready meals* jishishipin
*receipt* fapiao, shouju
*reception* (party, etc)
  jiedaishi
  (hotel, etc)
  jiedaichu
*record* (music)
  changpian
*red* hong
*red tea* hongcha
*refrigerator* bingxiang
*religion* zongjiao
*rent* (for room, etc)
  fangzu
  (verb) zu
  *for rent* chuzu
*repair* xiuli

*report* (noun)
  baogaoshu
*request* (noun)
  qingqiu
*reservation* yuding
*restaurant* canguan
*return* (come back)
  fanhui
  (give back) huan
*return ticket*
  wanfanpiao
*rice* (cooked) mifan
  (uncooked) mi
*rice bowl* fanwan
*rice cooker* dianfanbao
*rice field* daotian
*rich* (person) hen
  youqian
*right* (not left) you
  *on the right* zai
  youbian
  (correct) dui
*ring* (on finger) jiezhi
*river* he
*road* lu
*roasted* kao
*rocks* yanshi
*roof* wuding, fangding
*room* (hotel, house)
  fangjian
  (space) kongjian
*room service* songcan
  fuwu
*rope* shengzi
*round* (adj) yuande
*rubber* (material)
  xiangjiao
*rubber band*
  songjindai
*rubbish* laji
*ruins* feixu
*run* pao
*Russia* eguo

# S

*sad* shangxin
*safe* (not in danger)
  ping an
  (not dangerous)
  anquan
*safety pin* biezhen
*salad* sela
*sales* (company)
  xiaoshou
*salt* yan

*same* yiyang
  *the same again, please*
  zai lai yige
*sand* sha
*sandals* liangxie
*sandwich* sanmingzhi
*sanitary towels*
  weishengjin
*satellite TV* weixing
  dianshi
*Saturday* xingqiliu
*sauce* jiang
*sausage* xiangchang
*say: how do you say …
  in Chinese*
  yong hanyu zenme
  shuo …?
*school* xuexiao
*science* (study) li-ke
*scissors* jiandao
*Scotland* sugelan
*screen* pingmu
*screwdriver* luosidao
*sea* hai
*seafood* haixian
*seat* zuowei
  *take a seat* zuo
*seat belt* anquandai
*second* (in series) di er
  (of time) miao
*secretary* mishu
*section* (of shop)
  difang
*see* kanjian
  *I see!* shi zheyang!
*self-employed* getihu
*sell* mai
*seminar* zuotanhui
*separately* (pay) fen
  kai fu
*September* jiuyue
*serious* (illness)
  yanzhong
*sesame oil* mayou
*set* (theatre) bujing
*seven* qi, qi-ge
*shade: in the shade*
  zai yinliang chu
*shampoo* xifajing
*shave* guahuzi
*shaving cream*
  tixugao
*she* ta
*sheep* yang
*sheet* (for bed)
  chuangdan

*ship* chuan

*shirt* chenshan

*shoelaces* xiedai

*shoes* xiezi

*shoeshop* xiedian

*shop* shangdian

*shopkeeper* dianzhu

*shopping* (activity) gouwu

*shopping trolley* shoutuiche

*short* ai
  (time) duan

*shorts* duanku

*shoulder* jianbang

*shower* (in bathroom) linyu

*shower gel* yuye

*shrimp* xia

*shut* guan

*shutter* chuangban

*Siberia* xiboliya

*siblings* xiongdi

*side street* xiaojie

*sight: the sights of…* fengjing…

*sightseeing* guanguang

*signature* qianming

*silk* sichou

*Silk Road* sichou zhi lu

*silver* yin

*sing* changge

*Singapore* xinjiapo

*single: I'm single* wo shi danshen

*single room* danren fang

*single ticket* danchengpiao

*sink* shuichi

*sister (older)* jiejie
  *(younger)* meimei

*sit* zuo

*six* liu, liu-ge

*skirt* qunzi

*sky* tian kong

*sleep* shuijiao

*sleeper coach* yingwo chexiang

*sleeve* xiuzi

*slippers* tuoxie

*slow(ly)* man

*small* xiao

*smell* (have bad smell)
  nanwende qiwei

*smile* (verb) xiao

*smoke* (noun) yan
  *do you smoke?* ni xiyan ma?

*snacks* xiaochi

*snake* she

*so: so good* zhenhao
  *not so much* buyao name duo

*soap* feizao

*socks* wazi

*socializing* shejiao

*sofa* shafa

*soft* (material, etc) ruan

*soft drink* (ruan) yinliao

*soil* (earth) tu

*sole* (of shoes) xiedi

*somebody* youren

*something* youxie dongxi

*sometimes* you shi

*somewhere* mouchu

*son* erzi

*song* ge

*soon* bu jiu

*sorry* duibuqi
  *sorry?* ni shuo shenme?

*soup* tang

*south* nan

*souvenir* jinianpin

*soy sauce* jiangyou

*speak* jiang

*spider* zhizhu

*spoon* tiaogeng, shaozi

*sport* tiyu

*spring* (season) chun

*spring onion* xiaocong

*square* guangchang

*stage* (theatre) wutai

*stairs* louti

*stamp* (for letter) youpiao

*stapler* dingshuji

*start* (noun) kaishi

*starters* toupan

*statement* (e.g. witness) zhengci

*station* (railway) huoche zhan

*steak* niupai

*steal: my bag has been stolen*
  wo-de bao bei tou le
  *what was stolen?* diushi le shenme?

*steamed* zheng

*steps* taijie

*sticky rice* nuomi

*stockings* changtongwa

*stomach* fu, duzi, wei

*stomachache* wei teng

*stones* shitou

*stop* (bus stop) chezhan
  *stop!* ting!
  *stop here* zai zheli ting

*storm* baofengyu

*stove* luzao

*straight; it's straight ahead* yizhi chaoqian
  *go straight on* zhaozhi zou

*street* jie

*string* xisheng

*student* xuesheng

*stupid* yuchun

*sugar* tang

*suit* (noun) xizhuang

*suitcase* xiangzi

*summer* xia

*Summer Palace* yiheyuan

*sun* taiyang

*sunblock* (cream) fangshairu

*sunburnt* shaiheide

*Sunday* xingqiri

*sunglasses* taiyangjing

*sunshade* yangsan

*sunstroke* zhongshu

*suntan lotion* fangshaiji

*supermarket* chaoji shichang

*suppository* shuanji

*sure: I'm sure* wo quexin
  *are you sure?* ni neng kending ma?

*sweat* (noun) han
  (verb) chuhan

*sweater* taoshan

*sweet* (adj) tian
  (confectionery) tangguo

*sweet and sour* tangcu

*sweltering: it's sweltering* menre

*swim* (verb) youyong

*swimming* youyong

*swimsuit* youyongyi

*swimming pool* youyongchi

*swimming trunks* youyongku

*syringe* zhusheqi

*syrup* (medicinal) tangjiang

# T

*table* zhuozi

*table tennis* pingpang

*tablets* yaopian

*Taiwan* taiwan

*take* (transport) cheng (someone somewhere) dailing (something somewhere) dai

*talk* (verb) shuohua

*tall* gao

*tampons* miansai

*Taoism* daojiao

*tap* shuilongtou

*tape* (cassette) cidai (invisible adhesive) touming jiaodai

*taxi* chuzuche

*taxi rank* chuzuche zhan

*tea* cha
 *tea with milk* naicha

*teacher* laoshi

*telegram* dianbao

*telephone* dianhuaji, dianhua
 *telephone card* dianhua ka, IP ka
 *telephone number* dianhua haoma

*television* dianshi

*tell* gaosu

*temperature* (weather) qiwen
 (fever) fashao

*temple* miao

*tent* zhangpeng

*terminal* (airport, etc.) houjilou

*Terracotta Army* bingmayong

*terrible* zhen zaogao

*test* (hospital) huayan

*Thailand* taiguo

*than* bi ... geng
 *smaller than* bi ... xiao

*thank you* xiexie (ni)

*that: that woman* neige nvren
 *that man* neige nanren
 *what's that* na shi shenme?

*theatre* juchang, juyuan

*their(s)* tamen-de

*them* tamen

*theme park* zhutigongyuan

*then* (after that) ranhou
 (at that time) na shi

*there* nali
 *there is/are* you... *is/are there...?* you... ma?
 *there isn't/aren't ...* mei you...

*thermos flask* reshuiping

*these* zhexie

*they* tamen

*thick* hou

*thief* pashou

*thin* (thing) bao
 (person) shou

*thing* dongxi

*think* xiang

*thirsty: I'm thirsty* wo kouke

*this: this street* zhe tiao jie
 *this one* zhege
 *what's this?* zhe shi shenme?

*thousand* qian
 *ten thousand* wan

*those* naxie

*three* san, san-ge

*throat* houlong

*through* Jingguo

*thunderstorm* leiyu

*Thursday* xingqisi

*Tibet* xizang

*ticket* piao
 *admission ticket* menpiao
 *train/bus ticket* chepiao
 *airline ticket* jipiao

*tie* (around neck) lingdai

*tiger* hu

*tights* kuwa

*time* shijian
 *next time* xia ci
 *on time* zhundian
 *what time is it?* xianzai ji dian le?

*timetable* shijianbiao

*tip* (money) xiaofei

*tired* lei

*tissues* shouzhi

*to* dao
 *to England* qu yinggelan

*toast* (bread) kao mianbaopian

*today* jintian

*tofu* doufu

*tofu shop* doufudian

*together* yiqi

*toilet* cesuo

*toilet paper* weishengzhi

*tomato* xihongshi

*tomorrow* mingtian

*tonic* (water) kuangquanshui

*tonight* jintian wanshang

*too* (also) ye
 (excessively) tai

*tooth* ya

*toothache* ya teng

*toothbrush* yashua

*toothpaste* yagao

*tour* (noun) lvxing

*tourist* lvxingzhe

*tourist information office* lvyou fuwu zhongxin

*towel* maojin

*town* chengzhen

*traditional* chuantong

*traffic lights* hong lv deng

*train* huoche

*transformer* bianyaqi

*translate* fanyi

*travel agent* lvxingshe

*traveller's cheque* lvxingzhipiao

*travelling* lvyou

*tree* shu

*trip* (journey) lvxing

*trolley* shoutuiche

*trousers* kuzi, chang ku

*true* zhende

*try* (test) shi shi

*T-shirt* duanxiu yuanling hanshan

*Tuesday* xingqier

*turn* zhuan
  *turn left* zuo zhuan
  *turn right* you zhuan

*two* er, liang-ge

*tweezers* niezi

*tyre* chetai, luntai

## U

*umbrella* yusan

*uncle* shushu

*under* zai ... xiamian

*underground* (metro) ditie

*underground station* ditie zhan

*unfortunately* kexi

*United States* meiguo

*university* daxue

*university lecturer* daxuejiangshi

*urgent* jizhen

## V

*vaccination* yufangjiezhong

*vanilla* xiangcao

*vase* huaping

*vegetables* shucai

*vegetarian* sushizhe

*very* hen, feichang

*very well* (OK) haoba

*video games* dianzi youxi

*video tape* luxiangdai

*Vietnam* yuenan

*view* (scenery) jingse

*village* cunzhuang

*violin* xiaotiqin

*visa* qianzheng

*visit* (place) canguan
  (people) baifang

*visiting hours* tanwang shijian

*voice* shengyin

*voicemail* liuyanji

*voltage* dianya

*vomit* (verb) outu

## W

*wait* deng

*waiter* zhaodai

*waiting room* (clinic) houzhenshi

*waitress* nvzhaodai

*Wales* wei'ershi

*wall* qiang
  *the Great Wall of China* changcheng

*wallet* qianbao

*walk, go for a walk* sanbu

*want: I want* wo yao

*ward* (hospital) bingfang

*warm* nuanhuo

*washing machine* xiyiji

*washing powder* xiyifen

*washing-up liquid* xijiejing

*wasp* huangfeng

*watch* (wrist) shoubiao
  (verb) kan

*water* shui

*we* women

*weather* tianqi

*web site* wangzhan

*wedding* hunli

*Wednesday* xingqisan

*week* xingqi

*welcome* huanying
  *you're welcome* bu keqi

*well: I don't feel well* wo ganjue bushufu

*west* xi

*Western-style* xishi

*wet* shi

*what?* shenme?

*wheel* lunzi
  (vehicle) chelun

*wheelchair* lunyi

*when?* shenme shihou?

*where?* na'er?, nali?

*where: where is ...?* ... zai nali?

*which: which one?* na yige?

*whisky* weishiji

*white* bai

*who?* shei?
  *who's calling?* nin shi shei ya?

*why?* wei shenme?

*wide* kuan

*wife* qizi

*wind* feng

*window* chuanghu

*windscreen* dangfengboli

*wine* putaojiu
  *wine list* jiushui dan

*wing mirror* houshijing

*winter* dong

*with* he ...

*without* meiyou

*witness* zhengren

*woman* nvren, nvshi

*women's toilets* nv cesuo

*wood* mutou

*wool* yangmao

*word* ci

*work* (noun) gongzuo
  (verb) gongzuo
  *it's not working* huaile

*worktop* chutai

*worry: don't worry* bie danxin

*wrench* huo banshou

*write* xie
  *could you write it down?* ni neng bu neng xie yixia?

*wrong* cuo

## X

*X-ray* x-guang

## Y

*Yangtze Gorges* changjiang sanxia

*Yangtze River* changjiang

*year* nian

*yellow* huang

*Yellow River* huanghe

*Yellow Sea* huanghai

*yes* shide
*yesterday* zuotian
*yet: not yet* hai meine
*yoghurt* suannai
*you* ni
  (formal) nin
  (plural) nimen
*young* nianqing
*your(s)* ni-de
  (plural) nimen-de

# Z

*zip* lalian
*zoo* dongwuyuan

# The Chinese writing system

## Introduction

Chinese characters evolved from pictograms. These crude drawings originally resembled the object or idea they referred to (for example, an animal or a natural feature). In this way, Chinese writing developed as a series of ideograms, or characters, and not as an alphabet. But over time the characters became more complex. In modern Chinese, a few characters still bear a discernable likeness to the object they refer to, but most have changed beyond recognition.

Unlike an alphabet, Chinese characters do not carry an immediate clue as to their pronunciation – you can't look at one as a beginner and know (or even guess) how to say it. Each character needs to be learnt individually. This may at first seem like a daunting task, and no-one would pretend it is a fast process. On the other hand, when you understand how the Chinese language combines basic concepts to produce more complex ideas, you will see that even a few basic characters can take you a long way.

The purpose of this section is to show how you can start to decipher the characters, beginning with the simplest and most common. Writing the characters is another skill and one for which you will need a specialist book showing the order and direction of the strokes making up each character.

## Traditional and simplified characters

During the 1950s and 1960s, the People's Republic of China (mainland China) developed a simplified set of Chinese characters in an effort to promote literacy amongst the general population. The number of strokes in many characters was reduced and the shape simplified.

The simplified set of characters is used today in the PRC, although some other Chinese-speaking regions, notably Taiwan, still use the traditional set. *15-Minute Chinese* uses simplified characters as this is the most useful set for beginners to learn.

## *Basic concepts*

Some basic concepts and natural features are represented by a single character, and the simplest of these are the easiest characters to recognize at first.

### Numbers

The basic Chinese characters representing number are easily recognized. The characters for the numbers one to five also show the significance of the number and order of the strokes (see Read it box page 14).

| | | | |
|---|---|---|---|
| 一 | yi *(one)* | 六 | liu *(six)* |
| 二 | er *(two)* | 七 | qi *(seven)* |
| 三 | san *(three)* | 八 | ba *(eight)* |
| 四 | si *(four)* | 九 | jiu *(nine)* |
| 五 | wu *(five)* | 十 | shi *(ten)* |

Once you can recognize and say these characters, you can combine them to produce higher numbers:

十一   shiyi *(eleven – "ten one")*

十二   shier *(twelve – "ten two")*

十九   shijiu *(nineteen – "ten nine")*

八十   bashi *(eighty – "eight ten")*

四十   sishi *(forty – "four ten")*

六十五   liushiwu *(sixty-five – "six ten five")*

Add one more character and you can recognize all the months of the year:

三月　　sanyue *(March – "three month")*

七月　　qiyue *(July – "seven month")*

十一月　　shiyiyue *(November – "eleven month")*

And another one to tell the time:

四点　　sidian *(four o'clock – "four point")*

八点　　badian *(eight o'clock – "eight point")*

十二点　　shierdian *(twelve o'clock – "twelve point")*

The same principle works with the days of the week and other numerical concepts. So with just 12 characters, you can already recognize dozens of words.

## Natural features

Some of the first pictograms to develop were probably those representing natural features (e.g. *river, mountain, horse,* etc.). They are still amongst the simplest and most memorable characters, sometimes retaining a resemblance to the original concept (see *mountain, tree,* and *person,* for example).

山　san *(mountain)* 　　水　shui *(water)*

树　shu *(tree)* 　　土　tu *(soil)*

羊　yang *(sheep)* 　　马　ma *(horse)*

人　ren *(person)* 　　鱼　yu *(fish)*

## Basic grammatical words

Some characters representing basic grammatical concepts recur frequently:

我　wo (I)　　你　ni (you)

他　ta (he)　　她　ta (she)

是　shi (am/are/is)　　的　de (of/belonging to)

们　men (plural indicator)

If you learn to recognize these seven basic characters, the literal nature of Chinese means that you will be able to recognize a vocabulary equivalent to over three times as many English words (*I, you, he, she, we, they, my, your, his, her, our, their, mine, yours, ours, theirs, me, him, I'm, you're, we're, she's*, etc.), for example:

我们　women (we)　　他们　tamen (they)

我的　wo-de (my)　　你的　ni-de (your)

我们的　women-de (our)

## Other common characters

There are other commonly recurring Chinese characters that will open the door to entire vocabulary sets for you, for example:

大　da (big)　　小　xiao (small)

车　che (vehicle)　　机　ji (machine)

店　dian (shop)　　好　hao (good/well)

晚　wan (late/evening)　　早　zao (early/morning)

餐　can (meal)　　很　hen (very)

You can often find these characters in combination with others. Here are a few examples from *15-Minute Chinese*:

早餐    zaocan *(breakfast – "early meal")*

晚餐    wancan *(dinner – "late meal")*

餐馆    canguan *(restaurant– "meal place")*

你好    nihao *(hello – "you well")*

很好    henhao *(very good)*

早上好    zaoshang hao *(good morning – "early time good")*

晚上好    wanshang hao *(good evening – "late time good")*

出租车    chuzuche *(taxi – "hire vehicle")*

火车    huoche *(train – "fire vehicle")*

车票    chepiao *(ticket – "vehicle fare")*

小胡子    xiaohuzi *(moustache – "small beard")*

小路    xiaolu *(path – "small road")*

小吃    xiaochi *(snacks – "small eat")*

大学    daxue *(university – "big school")*

鞋店    xiedian  *(shoe shop)*

书店    shudian *(bookshop)*

飞机    feiji  *(plane – "flying machine")*

复印机    fuyinji  *(photocopier – "photocopy machine")*

## Summary

Understanding the principle of how the Chinese script works will enable you to break down a string of characters representing a word or phrase. It will help you identify familiar and unfamiliar characters. For example, look at the following sentence from the first conversation in *15-Minute Chinese*:

你好，我的名字是韩红。

*(Hello. My name's Han Hong.)*

Because you are now familiar with some basic characters, you can identify the characters that mean "hello", "my", and "is". You can also deduce the characters for "name" (名字 mingze) and "Han Hong" (韩红). More importantly, you will understand better the structure of the Chinese sentence (literally "you well. I-belonging to name is Han Hong").

Look back over other words and phrases in *15-Minute Chinese* and do your own detective work. You will realize that every word and phrase does not have to be learnt in isolation. The common characters with their shared sounds and meanings will help you build your Chinese vocabulary.

# Useful signs

Here are some useful signs you may see around you in China. Try to apply the principle of breaking down the combinations into their component characters to help you to recognize them. You will also find common road signs on pp.44–5.

入口
rukou
*Entrance*

出口
chukou
*Exit*

厕所
cesuo
*Toilets*

男厕所
nancesuo
*Men's toilet*

女厕所
nvcesuo
*Women's toilet*

出口
weixian
*Danger*

禁止吸烟
jinzhi xiyan
*No smoking*

警察局
jingchaju
*Police station*

医院
yiyuan
*Hospital*

银行
yinhang
*Bank*

动提款机
zidong tikuanji
*Cash point*

邮局
youju
*Post office*

火车站
huoche zhan
*Train station*

机场
jichang
*Airport*

# Acknowledgments

The publisher would like to thank the following for their help in the preparation of this book: Tamlyn Calitz for editorial assistance, Capel Manor College, Toyota (GB), Magnet Kitchens Kentish Town, Xerox UK, Wei Wei Zhu, Hannah Ho, Lik-Chung Li, Teresa Miao, Dave Wong, Oliver Stockdale, and Clive Moset.

Language content for Dorling Kindersley by G-AND-W PUBLISHING
Managed by **Jane Wightwick**

Picture research: **Lee Riches**
Illustration: **Hugh Schermuly and Lee Riches**

## Picture credits

**Key:**
t=top; b=bottom; l=left; r=right; c=centre; A=above; B=below

p1 DK Images: Wu Ming c; p2/3 DK Images: Colin Sinclair l; p4/5 DK Images: tcl; Colin Sinclair tl, Linda Whitwam tr, Howard Rice br; Ingram Image Library: tcr; Alamy: mediacolor's bcl; p6/7 Laura Knox: cl; p14/15 DK Images: Paul Bricknell cAl; Ingram Image Library: cbl, cAr; p16/17 Ingram Image Library: ctr; p18/19 DK Images: David Murray tr; Andy Crawford cll; p22/23 Alamy: Robert Harding Picture Library Ltd cl; Alamy: mediacolor's tcr; p24/25 Alamy: Charlie Lim cl; DK Images: Wu Ming bl, Ingram Image Library: tcr; p28/29 DK Images: John Bulmer tcr; Alamy: Christophe Testi cr; Ingram Image Library: bcr; p30/31 Alamy RF: Comstock Images bcl; DK Images: c; Alamy: Ferruccio cr; p34/35 Takehisa Yano: tcr; Alamy: Kevin Foy tBr; Alamy: Charlie Lim cr;p36/37 DK Images: cbr; p38/39 DK Images: Wu Ming bl-r, Alamy: Ulana Switucha c; Alamy: Mike Goldwater tcr; Alamy: Dbimages cr; p40/41 Alamy: David Robinson/Snap2000 Images cl, DK Images: Karen Trist © Rough Guides bl, DK Images: Bryn Walls tcr, tcrB, cr, br DK Images: Colin Sinclair cAr Alamy: David Robinson/Snap2000 Images bcrA; p42/43 DK Images: Wu Ming bl-r, cr, DK Images: Bryn Walls c, tcr, tcrB, crB DK Images: Colin Sinclair crA; p44/45 Courtesy of Toyota (GB): c; p46/47 Toyota (GB): tr; Ingram Image Library: cAr; DK Images: Bryn Walls tcl,cr, DK Images: Colin Sinclair bl, Images: Karen Trist © Rough Guides cr, Alamy: Ulana Switucha br; p48/49 DK Images: cl, c, bcl, bcr, Linda Whitwam tcr, Chris Stowers clA, Alamy: JTB Photo Communications r; p60/61 Alamy RF: Image Source cBr, cr DK Images: Bryn Walls bl; Steve Gorton cAAr; Pia Tryde cAr, bcr; p62/63 DK Images: Wu Ming bl-r, c; Jo Foord cr; Andy Crawford crA; Geoff Brightling crB; p64/65 DK Images: c; Alamy: Arcaid bcr; Alamy RF: Diana Ninov cAr; Ingram Image Library: tcr; p66/67 Alamy: Arcaid cll; DK Images: Wu Ming bc; Ingram Image Library: bcr; Alamy RF: Image Source cr; p68/69 DK Images: cBr, Wu Ming clAl, cll, clBr, cbr; Geoff Brightling bl; Hugh Sykes: clAr, cl, clBl, ctr, cAr; p70/71 DK Images: Wu Ming bl-r; p72/73 Alamy RF: Comstock Images tcr; Hugh Sykes: tcrB; Alamy: Belinda Lawley crA; Tina Manley/Business cr; p74/75 Alamy RF: Doug Norman bl; p76/77 DK Images: Wu Ming bcd, bcAll, bcAlll,cbr; Hugh Sykes: bcll, bcAll, bcAl; p80/81 Getty: Taxi / Rob Melnychuk bc; Ingram Image Library: cAr; Xerox UK Ltd: tcr; p82/83 Alamy: jack Sullivan tcr; Alamy RF: Momentum Creative Group cAl; Ingram Image Library: cl; p84/85 DK Images: bl; Alamy RF: SuperStock tr; Brand X Pictures cr; Ingram Image Library: crB; p86/87 Getty: Taxi / Rob Melnychuk tc; DK Images: bcrA, Wu Ming bcrAA; p88/89 DK Images: Wu Ming bl-r, Alamy: Ace Stock Limited br; p90/91 DK Images: cl; David Jordan cAr; Stephen Oliver cr; Ingram Image Library: cBr; p92/93 Ingram Image Library: cl; Alamy RF: Pixland cr; DK Images: Guy Ryecart tr; p94/95 Alamy RF: ImageState Royalty Free bcr; DK Images: tcr; p96/97 DK Images: ctl; p98/99 Getty Images: Daisuke Morita c; DK Images: Frank Greenaway bcl; p100/101 DK Images: Steve Gorton tcr; p102/103 DK Images: Peter Chen bl; Andrew butler tcr; Bruce Forster tcrB; Linda Whitwam cr; Howard Rice crA; p104/105 DK Images: Bob Langrish cl(5); Jane Burton bcl; Max Gibbs cl(3); Frank Greenaway cl(2); Tracy Morgan c(4); Dave King cl(1); p106/107 Getty Images: Daisuke Morita cr; DK Images: bcr; p110/111 Alamy RF: Stockbyte tl; Ingram Image Library: bl; Alamy: Real World People tcrB; Geoff A Howard cl; p114/115 Alamy: View Stock cl; Ace Stock Limited cr; DK Images: Linda Whitwam tcr; p116/117 DK Images: Wu Ming bcr; Alamy: Geoff A Howard clA; p118/119 Alamy RF: Stock Image/Pixland br; DK Images: Courtesy of the Chinese Opera Institute, Singapore c; p120/121 Alamy: ImageState cl; DK Images: bcl; p122/123 DK Images: Judith Miller / Sparkle Moore at The Girl Can't Help It cl; Alamy: Geoff A Howard c; p124/125 DK Images: Bob Langrish ctr(3); Max Gibbs cl(4); Frank Greenaway clA(2); Tracy Morgan cr(5); Dave King cll(1); Alamy: ImageState bclA; DK Images: bcl; p126/127 DK Images: Wu Ming cl, cll, clll; Ingram Image Library: brAA; Alamy: David Crausby br; p128 DK Images: Neil Mersh tl.

All other studio and location images **Mike Good**